Strangers to

Nita Lindenberg

Strangers to themselves

Encounters with retarded and insane people

Floris Books

Translated by Ruth M. Whittchow

Originally published in German under the title
Sich selber fremd by Verlag Urachhaus in 1969.
First published in English by Floris Books in 1989.

British Library CIP Data

Lindenberg, Nita
Strangers to themselves: Encounters with
retarded and insane people
1. Germany. Mentally ill persons.
Biographies. Collection
I. Title   II. Sich selber fremd. *English*
362.2′092′2

ISBN 0–86315–087–X

Printed in Great Britain
by Camelot Press plc, Southampton

Contents

Foreword

When in the fifties the laws pertaining to mental disorder were adapted and changed, the long history of misunderstanding the retarded and mentally ill person took a positive turn. In 1957 the proposed new terminology was aimed at eliminating the words 'idiot' and 'imbecile' or 'mental defective', and authorities began to question the ineducability of the subnormal person, hitherto determined through one-sided methods of testing. It is difficult to imagine what the general outlook on the so-called deranged person was fifty years earlier when young Nita von Kügelgen gained her early experience; and how futuristic an institution her father had developed over against the generally held views. Even in the first decades of this century only a very few enlightened pioneers dared to bring the mentally handicapped sector into closer touch with society at large, and encourage open discussion. Many of the encounters told in this book took place when no platforms of sharing existed such as parents' associations or conferences for special education. Most forms of professional training, for those working with mentally retarded or insane people, were only developed after the middle of this century and with this came a greater understanding of the special child, the handicapped adult and the mentally ill.

Nita will soon celebrate her ninetieth birthday, and remains active in helping to change conditions that only now approach a more realistic social integration of those strangers in this world.

The first stories come from a now lost world of Estonia, then a province of Tsarist Russia. We are led with Nita Lindenberg and her companions through Japan and Russia in the turbulent days of war and the Russian Revolution, and later live through the shattered existence of World War Two. Most of the events recounted in the last chapter of the book took place in the fifties and sixties. Listening today to the fount of stories from this remarkable lady one realizes that her encounters with human beings from all walks of life, with varying needs, have continued far beyond the writing of this book in 1965.

Living now with her husband, a minister of The Christian Community, in her chosen homeland of Southern Germany, she continues to serve the needs of the time. At present she is the driving force to save a rare stretch of woodland near her local village from industrial exploitation, never in her life has her fighting spirit left her. She can recall her days in Cologne in the early sixties when she was in charge of a day school for handicapped children, while she completed her remedial education training. Before that she was responsible for a state home for retarded children in Bavaria. One of her innovative contributions was her involvement with the 'school-bridge' principle to enable slow learners and handicapped children to make the step into higher education with dignity. Prior to this lay a time of intense educational and curative pedagogical activity in her own home and its surrounding. In Germany during the Second World War she managed, with a fire, courage and determination defying all hostile authorities, to build a house in a rural setting. This became a home for her own and other children, and a haven for politically and racially persecuted children, some of whom were emotionally disturbed. What was established under a mantle of secrecy could, after the War, flourish and grow.

In 1929 she was directing her own sanatorium south of Dresden, working with anthroposophically orientated doctors. There she met her present husband with whom she had six children. Before this, after her voluntary departure from Estonia in 1919 came ten years of varied experience in the world; a nurse's training in Berlin, a marriage with two children, life in an old castle managing the estate and finally directing two sanatoriums in the Black Forest and Saxonia respectively.

Through her own words we meet Nita Lindenberg's unusual childhood and youth, which was so deeply influenced by her father. Unmentioned are the years of political exile in the wilds of Siberia, three hundred miles from the nearest railway station; her education in a private boarding school in Japan. Her birth in St Petersburg (Leningrad) eluded even the anxious publisher of this edition's cover!

Although Nita Lindenberg wrote another book in 1979 and still today lets the ink flow, she never claims to be a writer in the literary sense. Challenging the reader with a brisk aphoristic style to catch the unspoken controversies, she remains the same as in personal contact, compelling attention and letting the one main motive shine through her descriptions: to make a difference with each encounter.

Christof-Andreas and Norma Lindenberg
Camphill Village Kimberton Hills 1989

And when the bear hurried through the half open door he got caught on the latch, and a piece of his fur was torn open. Through the hole which was made in his coat Snow-White thought she saw the glittering of gold, but she was not quite certain about it.

The Brothers Grimm, *Snow-White and Rose-Red*

I

In the Beginning

These stories of the 'mentally disturbed' have been set down in order to strengthen our certainty. I want to reveal the gold beneath the bear's skin, the indestructible, the human image.

The man in the street does not say 'mentally ill' he says 'mad', 'deranged', when referring to a person in whom nothing is in its proper place, either in the reason or in the emotions. People say, 'demented', because aim and purpose are no longer there; the mentally deranged person gropes in the dark. He also says 'insane' when the sense of right and wrong, of hot and cold, has gone astray. He says that a person is 'crazy' when the obsession with a fixed idea never wavers. He says 'imbecile' and 'simple minded' when life's diversity is no longer reflected in the afflicted person. 'Mentally ill,' however, a synthetic term, is not used by the man in the street. The spirit cannot be ill any more than it can die.

I remember a walk through the city park with twenty-five children from the home, the little patients in the middle, the kindergarten nurses on the outside like Alsatian dogs, patient and alert. The footsteps of the mentally handicapped children dragged and faltered oddly as though they were rustling through undergrowth.

'Taking your apes for a walk?' an elderly couple

shouted. Two elderly gentlemen, professors perhaps, came to a standstill: 'Incredible! are such children not kept fenced off?' Twenty-five pairs of eyes stared at the gentlemen penetratingly, as if making detailed observations, yet looked beyond them as though their thoughts had become materially visible. Two mothers hustled children with dolls' prams and sand-pit pie dishes out of the way. A doll was left lying. 'Go and give it to the little girl', the kindergarten nurse said, so our Bimbo took the doll carefully by the legs and carried it over to the child clinging to her mother. 'No, let it be!' cried the mother, 'You cannot have the doll anymore. I will buy you a new one, that one is dirty now.'

Upon our return to the Home, it is Abel who responds to the experience. Up until now he had only spoken one sentence; for thirteen years just one sentence, 'Little flowers blossom.' He used to go along the corridor with a watering can, spraying water over the floor saying, 'Little flowers blossom.' The medical attendant asked his name and he replied, 'little flowers blossom.' Even during the six months he had been in the Home he had not learned any other answer but 'Little flowers blossom.' Now, after the walk, he comes to the kindergarten nurse, puts his arms around her, lays his head on her shoulder and asks, 'Am I cuckoo?'

It was then I resolved to tell the stories of the 'insane', both great and small. These stories are of immense importance. Is not our life poverty stricken because we are so 'normal', cut off and separated from the wondrous worlds of those souls held captive by insanity's enchantment? They have really lived, or are still alive, and they ask, 'Am I cuckoo?'

Where it was, when it happened, as far as places and names are concerned, I have blended everything together. No-one will be recognized, no-one will be offended, yet everything really happened.

2

The Pioneer

The 'Seewald Clinic for the emotionally and mentally ill' was founded at the turn of the century, to my knowledge, by a group of philanthropists from the Baltic states. My father, then studying the latest research in Heidelberg, was utterly dismayed when he saw many purpose-built houses already standing, without his advice having been asked: a large boiler house for lighting, heating and pumping up water out of the deepest artesian well in the country, as well as a kitchen, wash-house, office, stables, two doctors' houses, a chapel, servants' quarters and two hospitals. He would have preferred to have had them pulled down, because the barrack-like style of the buildings was enough to frighten any patient, even before entering. He then did his utmost to improve the outer appearance by creating a homely atmosphere in all the halls and sick-rooms. He had beautiful lithographs sent from Germany, and hung those pictures even where they were often broken by the aggressive patients and so had to be replaced. The beds were covered with very colourful woollen blankets woven by the patients, similar to those

13

customary in the countryside. The attendants wore pink striped overalls, and the doctors did not wear white coats. The windows were not barred, the square kilometre of land around the clinic was not fenced in, and the entrance from the road was a large, open wooden gate with only the name Seewald as indication. One could not possibly feel afraid when entering the rural but well-cared grounds of Seewald. I believe that it was at that time the only mental institution in Europe where there were no padded cells, strait-jackets and the like.

Expansion was urgently needed. New ideas coming from Germany stimulated my father to plan beautifully formed buildings incorporating a sense of light and movement. The result was four new houses with space for over a thousand beds, which attracted visitors from near and far.

One day, a gentleman entered the grounds and asked us, then children, which building one could already visit. We told him: straight ahead for five hundred metres and the first new building on the right. An hour later the gentleman returned delighted, saying that he had now really seen the most modern of modern clinics: 'The large skylights, low walls perfect for easy supervision, the practical cooking area in the centre of the house, and the clean white basin fitted out so that food can be pushed along!' Our teacher burst out laughing, and we realized what had happened — the guest had been inspecting the new sty intended for three hundred and fifty pigs which, without its occupants, certainly did look 'modern'.

Other buildings followed: two doctors' villas designed in the Swedish style with wood, and a theatre where patients could perform, celebrate and, above all, learn Isadora Duncan dancing. My Father was severely criticized for the latter by the conservative Baltic people because one danced barefoot! A new, daring element had entered the clinic through the Duncan School in Berlin for educating mind, body and soul.

It is true that the most dangerous patients were lodged in two closed houses; one for men and one for women, with their own spacious gardens. The other houses — two for the 'infirm' (which means incurable), one for active patients who worked at joinery, weaving and other crafts, and one for the more elegant 'sanatorium cases' — were always open to me as a child. Here I would see my father, who was often so strict with us, radiating love with his whole being. His appearance alone was authoritative, but what the patients surely felt most was that he could 'see into them,' as our old head-attendant, Hergauk, once said.

Here I received a basic training without ever being taught directly; through watching my father at work I absorbed something which later made it possible for me, in so many different countries, to discover, understand and love my sick fellow-human beings as I had loved my childhood companions.

3

Childhood Experiences with Insane People

Even at the age of four, I was allowed to visit some sections of the clinic of which my father was the director. In fact, the patients were my friends and afforded me wonderful play companions; what splendid things they could do! Because I felt neither criticism nor disgust but, like my father, admired them and laughed with them, I was naturally accepted as one of themselves.

I made myself quite at home in the 'incurable' women's unit. The attendant in her striped uniform would come along rattling her bunch of keys to let me in. There sat Nenny on her bed again, about twenty small parcels lying round her as she relentlessly packed her bits and pieces. Every few weeks, the matron would take the whole pile away; where else would she find new material to give Nenny, who begged unremittingly for more? Yet all the parcels contained were bits of old rags and paper . . . I pounced on the scattered parcels, 'Let me pack too, Nenny, please!' Surrounded by the shadowy forms of the other patients, we wrapped and packed until the large jam sandwiches were brought in for elevenses.

I went over to Trino to hold her baby while she

drank coffee. Trino's baby was nothing other than her own pillow, but no-one knew better than I that the most important things are always invisible. I rocked him gently and we talked about how pretty and good he was, and how he was already quite plump like a little round apple. Trino, for her part, forgot that at four years of age, I could not as yet know much about a mother's duties; we felt united in our care and love.

The most beautiful of all was Mrs Glaser. The snowy locks above her intelligent, wrinkled face were far older than the lively blue eyes which observed everything and yet never looked one full in the face. She used to greet me with a highly perfected curtsy and when I was older, she would also kiss my hand. For her there existed only princesses and kings. Everyone else, being but common folk, were passed over with exemplary graciousness. How fortunate it was that I was a princess in her eyes! She often came to our house to help, as did Linda whom, throughout my childhood, I tried to cure of her silly laughter. She was always hopping and grinning. 'Oh Linda, I think you're stupid.' 'No, Nita Preili [Missy Nita], I'm very clever!'

I was not allowed in the men's unit. Yet that was where my very best friends lived. Take for instance Mr Schneiderovsky who made a mushroom garden beside the new forestry plantation. He put beech twigs and oak leaves, different soils and several kinds of herbs all together and, just imagine, juicy boletus, hard brown mushrooms, golden yellow saffron and milk caps all grew as if they had been sown and were ready for harvesting immediately. His secret he took to the grave. Until then I had never heard that mush-

17

rooms, apart from champignons, could be thus cultivated.

Then there was 'Monkey Neuwald' who taught me my first English sentences from a small Prayer Book from which he used to read in English to 'the unredeemed creatures' — the animals in the stable: 'The Lord is my shepherd . . .' He was often troubled with severe stomach pains and, to my pride and joy, I discovered that I could relieve him of them. All he needed was one spoonful of raspberry juice from a small bottle with a long label on which I had scribbled in large childish letters, 'One dose of tooth powder and sugar three times a day.' And he was cured! This went so far that the matron would say, 'Nita, be so good as to give Monkey Neuwald something for his stomach. Your drops always help.' Sure enough, the faithfully administered remedy brought greater relief than when the disbelieving patient took genuine medicine.

There, too, was fat Jurri who had to stay in Seewald because he had pushed his mother-in-law into the oven. He was full of fun and good ideas. Sometimes my father would bring him an orange and throw it into his open mouth. Golden and round, it would disappear, peel and all, down his throat. He also liked eating the little frogs which hopped about on the paths. Towards the end of summer, I would catch a handful and he would swallow the wriggling morsels with obvious pleasure. Jurri was a magnificent field hand; it was a sight to see him in the oatfield, stripped to the waist and swinging the scythe until the stems rustled and swished. In winter he made brooms. Once my father sent him into town with a handcart full of birch switches tied with red ribbon to stand in front of the house where a misbe-having niece of his lived. Although the motto 'Never will a rod of wood teach the children to be good,' was familiar in our home, I do think that the cart piled with switches and ribbons, and the great giant between the shafts, did indeed intimidate the little rascal watching from the window. Everyone, includ-ing Jurri and the passers-by, had tremendous fun.

The winter of 1918 was a hungry and lean period for everyone owing to the German occupation. Jurri, however, knew how to provide for himself. It was his job to tend the fire under the boiler and he would catch rats and roast them for himself. His fat, round face, satisfied and comical, was all that people saw and it was only the expert who could recognize the demon of destruction lurking within his soul.

An especially remarkable figure was a little man whose task it was to sweep the paths. He imagined that he was a general or a king, but best of all, an engineer. We children sewed colourful epaulettes for him and decorated his threadbare cap with a cockade. His broom would change to sceptre, sword or gun as he earnestly saluted everyone who seemed worthy of his greeting. One day the dreaded governor, fol-lowed by a large retinue, arrived for an inspection. The 'engineer' stood by the carriage door and raised his broom smartly to his shoulder just as the import-ant gentleman was about to step down. Quick as a flash, he withdrew into the safety of his carriage! From then on the governor fought against the free Seewald education with all his might. 'This incident,' he maintained, 'was perfect proof of the "rebellion" and "danger" latent in these patients.' During the years of the Bolshevik Revolution the 'engineer' did, in fact, make use of his broom as a weapon: when a rabble-rouser was making inflammatory speeches against the Germans from a heap of sand, the 'engineer' swept her deftly from her high seat, and so had the final word.

But, alas, all my friends had to disappear, often for months, when their bad periods came upon them. Then they had to stay in the closed section, ill and confused and unable to recognize their Nita Preili any more. The secret was to observe when their bad periods were coming.

Once, when my sister and I were in a field filling our pockets with turnips, a strange man suddenly stepped out of the bushes and we realized immediately that his 'dark' period had overcome him. A tall alder stood at the edge of the field. Breathless with fear, we climbed to the top of the tree where we remained besieged until evening. Luckily, he was too big and heavy to climb up after us. We could survive because it was a warm day and we had our turnips. The man made dull, strange, spasmodic sounds, reminding us of a similar situation when we had escaped up a large oak tree from a bull which, in fury, repeatedly charged the trunk with his horns. In both cases the approaching evening and hunger drove the enemy back home.

Escape or common sense did not always help. The matron, who had long managed on the strength of her kindness, was once assaulted by a patient in the storeroom and chased round the table for one hour before help finally arrived. Even my father, who refused to have either padded cells or strait-jackets in the clinic, was once overpowered by an enormous young man who lay upon him while a second patient stood by grinning. Only my father's bear-like strength saved him that time.

It is not surprising then, that living in such a community, we children developed a certain calm with regard to unexpected events. One morning, as we went through the gate for school we were confronted by a stark naked man. Later we were told he was a bricklayer who suddenly tore off all his clothes high up on the scaffolding, announced that he was crazy and had to go to Seewald. He then ran through the streets not allowing anyone to hinder him from reaching his destination. We told him in quite a matter-of-fact way, 'Go straight on through the entrance to the second house on the right. That's where the office is, and you can be enrolled.' With that we continued on our way to school. The man, incidentally, remained in the clinic for many years.

Indeed, it was remarkable how psychopaths or emotionally disturbed people recognized in good time that they were endangered and instinctively knew that my father could help them. A spectacular example was the officer's wife whose husband had fallen in the Japanese War. There, in the Far East, she went mad. Like a migrating bird unerring in its direction, she travelled through the whole of Siberia and Russia, almost entirely on foot, dragging her shattered spirit and her husband's scimitar mile after mile across the vast country, until one day she stood with her sledge piled with junk — the scimitar on top, in front of our verandah, asking to be admitted. As the insane are considered to be holy by the Russians, she had received food and help wherever she went, until she arrived at the place whither her infallible inner voice had led her.

I remember one particular event from a later period. We were sitting in my father's room from where we could look along the birch avenue down to the sea, glimmering like a blue window over a kilometre away. Twice a year, the sun went down at exactly that spot and it was as if one were looking into the glory of heaven. We sat looking out and talking, our eyes following the road which led straight between the patches of lawn and limestone. Suddenly, we caught sight of a man, scantily dressed in the clinic tunic, running down the avenue with a throng of attendants chasing behind him. In a flash, I jumped down on to the road and stood in the runaway's path. I then grabbed him by the hand with the special nurse's grip and he stood stock still, breathless until the attendants reached us. My father and the guests had followed, among them my husband-to-be. Something like triumphant pride glowed in my heart; there was I, young and healthy, beside me a sick man. But I was a child no longer, and had forgotten how to live in the same world with the deranged.

After many years, I returned home as a wife and mother and went past the women's unit. There they were, my childhood friends banging on the windows in recognition. The attendant opened the door and once again I was surrounded, 'Nita Preili, princess . . .' the tears welled up in my eyes.

4
The Artist

Hands buried in his short, warm jacket, the massive figure would very slowly make his way down to the sea every morning, scowling grimly and scaring the children away. He preferred to remain standing at the edge of the forest, from where he could see the water in the bay glimmering blue and grey beyond the red of the pine tree trunks and branches clustered with needles. There he saw the pictures which he carried home within him; he never worked out of doors. He could be seen leaning silently against a leafless birch tree, staring at the violet and green shadows on the snow in the evening light. Or one would meet him beside the meadow where a cow stood up to her belly in grass, like a red poppy against the pale, northern sky. He was also to be found in the city, standing in front of a desolate house; the empty alley-way would seem even lonelier, even colder under his gaze.

Then there were days when he came in to join us, with the family sitting round the table listening to a story, and the light from the large lamp shining on the coppery hair of our teacher. All of this he took in and painted at home. He never used a paintbrush, but painted with his fingers and the palms of his hands, and he almost never spoke.

All this took place during his good days. When, however, his bad days overcame him and darkened his spirit, one had to be quick enough to rescue the valuable pictures. He cut, bit, ripped and destroyed many lovely pieces of work within seconds.

Often he had to spend many months in the closed section, where all traces of the man and the artist that had ever lived in him seemed to have been extinguished. He would lash out at the attendants, doctors, and other patients. Wild at himself, he often came within a hair's breadth of committing an ingenious suicide: his water glass splintered into a drink, his towel used as a gag, the leg of his bed poised on his Adam's-apple . . .

Then, like a sunrise, his good times would return one morning, although one still had to wait before he was allowed out. Canvas, palette and paints would all be brought forth. Would he pick them up or destroy them? If his bad days were definitely over he will throw himself to work in a frenzy. And then he was as shrewd as a gypsy, knowing the price of his pictures, and never selling them for less.

He had studied in Paris at the turn of the century, standing out for his own particular quality which had attracted attention and was never forgotten. I do not know what happened then to cause his illness. He was brought back to his own country, to our clinic. There he spent his life, until the final catastrophe of the Second World War swept over the land.

The Artist will live on in our memories: a part of nature with her storms, strength and purity. A man full of sympathy and the desire to help; would he otherwise, filled with a compassionate feeling for the earth, have squeezed out all his paints, tube by tube, smoothing over the stony country road, 'So that the wheels of the heavy carts don't hurt it'?

5

Clumpy

As a twelve-year-old I had occasionally heard of 'Clumpy' who lay in the unit where the completely helpless and incurable patients lived. I had listened with horror and fascination, even with a kind of anger in my heart, to whatever I was told about him: a strong, young farmer's lad suddenly smitten with an infection.

A terrible 'bewitchment' had taken place. Not only had the illness damaged the young man's reason, speech and hearing, said the attendants, but his limbs had also rotted away, his nose and ears were only holes, and he was blind. They fed him through a tube because his mouth was gone. His nickname, 'Clumpy,' was about the last effort of good will shown by the attendants. How could God permit this? Why was he alive? For the first time, although I knew and loved so many patients, something within me rebelled. Why? Why?

Then one day quite by chance, as I was hanging about nearby, I was able to visit Clumpy. His mother had arrived. She came every few years, and here she was again. Even for the long-accustomed attendants it was an embarrassing task to show the mother her son. 'Nita Preili,' said the attendant in charge, 'would you like to go in with Clumpy's mother? She is old and frail, and perhaps if Preili goes too it will be a little easier.'

The old mother bent down to put on her shoes; she had covered the long distance from her village barefoot. A large shawl enveloped her completely. I saw the thousands of wrinkles on her forehead and cheeks, the clear eyes, the worn hands, and I said to her in her native tongue, 'Come with me.' We followed the warden into the large room. My heart was beating fast; up till then I had only known the open wards, I had never been allowed to enter this unit and would never have got in but for the arrival of Clumpy's mother. So I was to see him now, the person who was not a person and yet had lived on and on for how many years now? Neither the old woman nor I were aware of the many beds and their occupants as we stopped by Clumpy's bed. Both of us saw only him. I clenched my fists as I looked at what was lying there. A short, broad 'Something'. One could see that there were no arms or legs, just a little skull like a piece of weathered limestone, and a chest that breathed.

On to this chest the old woman placed a small bundle, a cake or a ham perhaps, whatever the custom was to bring from the country. She always brought it. Her crooked fingers stroked the horrible little head, 'Marti, are you well? I bring you greetings from everyone at home.' Then she looked at me with shining eyes, 'Preili! . . . he smiled . . .'

6

The Child-Murderess

She had been a spoilt, little, young lady. In the morning when Lisa brought her hot chocolate she would twitter contentedly from between her silk sheets; one delightful day melted into another. The drive with Mámushka, her mother, to the Neva islands of St Petersburg, was a high-point in her existence. She felt so grown up, waving and calling out greetings; everyone was kind and friendly, even the black horses in front of the carriage who held down their warm muzzles to be stroked. Was there anything at all in that sheltered life that was arduous, serious or inhibiting? Were there any duties or problems? Reality consisted of pastries, knick-knacks, dancing and drives out, caresses and kisses from all the dear relatives, and a loud scream if a wish was not immediately fulfilled.

Then one day a tall man in a top hat came and talked with Pápushka. He drank wine with them all and when he left he kissed little Olya's hand. What a strange, tall man! However, that evening, her mother said to her, 'My little dove, Mr Bender came to ask for your hand in marriage, and so there is going to be a wedding soon.' Olya had seen many weddings; the bridal garland, the priest with a long beard, the beautiful prayers and the many, many carriages! Now she too was going to see what it was like, it would all take place just for her, and she clapped her hands.

The next time we met Olya she was called Olya Petrova Bender — a charming little devil with whom only Lisa, who followed her into her new life, could cope. She laughed and played when she and Lisa were alone, she trembled and cried when Mr Bender was at home trying with a firm hand to accustom her to her new duties. 'Lisa, Lisa, take me home!'

But she had become estranged from home. She could drive there on a visit with Mr Bender, but then would have to kiss Mámushka's hand. She was not allowed to run into the old nursery or into the kitchen, for she was a wife, a wife. 'Lisa, Lisa, let me be a little girl again!' But Lisa was busy making little garments, 'Tiny shirts for your child, Olya,' 'Then let me at least drive out.' Yes, Mr Bender had nothing against that. He had beautiful horses and was happy that Olya had a wish which he could easily satisfy. So now Olya went out driving for many hours each day along the River Neva or to the Fortress of St Peter or simply through the streets. Most of all, she liked to drive to her parents' house and back. Lisa, a black scarf round her head, sat beside her thin little mistress and worried.

One day, something dreadful happened. A drunkard fell in front of the carriage, the horses shied, and Olya was hurled out on to the street. From then on she knew nothing. She did not know how her child was born, she did not know how much pity and concern surrounded her. Finally, she took her first timid steps. Lisa gave the little son, wrapped in silk and lace, into her arms. She did not regard the crazed look or the restless manner of her young mistress. She thought only that now all would be well. Olya took her child and went to the tower room. The tower was high, and Olya was still weak, but she climbed and climbed, urged irresistibly upward by the desire to send her son back to the heaven from which he had come, away from Mr Bender, away from everything from which she suffered and found so alien. She arrived, breathless, at the top and saw nothing but blue, nothing but light. Into this she let her child fall.

I visited Mrs Bender in the clinic every day. She was nearly always in bed writing letters, embroidering, sewing. Everything was small and delicate, rows and rows of neat lines, rows and rows of neat stitches, but nothing was ever completed. Her cupboard was full of embroideries and papers which she watched over zealously. In turns she was happy and laughed, she was angry and cried. She often related how she drove on and on, hour after hour in a white dress, the carriage and horses and even the coachman were all in white. Then she told her biggest secret; how she had carried her small child up into the tower and how, from there, he had floated like a soap bubble into the sky, higher and higher, until she could see him no more. That was her favourite and most beautiful story and I, still a child, could not hear it often enough.

7

Old Karel

Old Karel lived on the estate of our favourite uncle in the Baltic states. He had been there long before uncle. The aged blacksmith would say to us, 'Karel? He was certainly never young. He was already old when I was a child, and even then he was crazy.'

Then there was the 'Old Hostel' in which some of the estate workers still lived. You could reach up to touch the enormous moss-covered shingle roof, because it sat on the ramshackle hut like a hat that is too big. In the evening, when the paraffin lamps or candles were lit you could see the small greenish windows light up under the eaves. Only Karel's window remained dark. In the summer, he would stay out till late, sitting on a little bench in front of the crooked door with a few of the old workers around him. They were waiting for Karel's deep and resounding roar of laughter which was so contagious that everyone became gripped in helpless laughter. But Karel did not laugh on their behalf, nor for any reason at all: he had no idea why he was laughing. His head, with its long thick hair which the black-smith's wife sometimes cut into a bob, could very well have been a model for a Barlach figure. His clothes were indefinable, smelly and sticky.

In winter, he would go to sleep at dusk, but during

the day, when he shuffled along in his old slippers like a giant, with an oily sheepskin thrown over his shoulders, then all would call him in — the cartwright, the blacksmith, the cowherd — 'Karel, come and sit with us.' So he would sit down near the joiner's bench, the men constantly glancing in his direction until the sleepy giant lifted his head and let out his booming laugh, drawing everyone along with him until the workshop vibrated with laughter.

As children we were very shy of him because he was so immensely big. Nevertheless, now and then we dared to call out to him, 'Karel, laugh!' He usually took no notice and continued his nap in some stable corner or other, on the bridge, in front of the distillery, or preferably during the winter, in the ox's stall where it was nice and warm. It could happen, however, that just at that moment his laughter was due and we were able to listen in close proximity to his magnificent 'Ho-ho-ho!' that made us tingle from top to toe.

Once I was among those who brought Karel his Christmas gifts. We carried a small tree with lighted candles, some bacon, cake and a bottle of mead. In this way I entered his room for the first time. Karel was too tall to stand upright in it, and in the pale gleam of the candles we saw his bowed shadow like an enormous St Christopher's silhouette on the wall. There was a box-bed with a straw mattress on which sheepskin lay, a table and stool with crooked legs, and nails on the wall with rope, rags and his fur cap hanging up. Through the half-open door of a heavy brick stove one could see the glow of burning turf. Karel was very disturbed by our arrival and waved at us with both hands, 'Out! Out!' so we hurriedly left after saying 'Happy Christmas' and laying down the presents. Outside, we wondered whether Karel knew how to deal with the candles on the Christmas tree, but we saw that it was already dark behind the windows. Dazzling light did not fit in with Karel's gloomy hut, but before we had reached the street we heard his deep laughter like thunder, 'Ho-ho-ho!' This time no-one joined him because people were celebrating with their families in their own homes.

Later, when I had learned something about the structure of society, I marvelled at the way in which, in bygone days, a sick old man would be supported by the community for decades. He received his daily bread and his peat for burning. Why was it given to him? Tradition and a sense of duty were certainly part of the answer but it was not only that Karel was a part of the estate. Did they not, at least subconsciously, fear this age-old legendary figure, left over from bygone mythical aeons who, powerfully tall and silent, concealed dull memories of the time when gnomes and giants still roamed among us? Was he 'remembering' when he laughed?

Once I was present at a St John's festival when Karel appeared unexpectedly. Together with the people of estate, we had lit the great midsummer fire. Large barrels of tar had been hoisted up to hang from between the trees and were set alight. A tall pole had been erected and on this the farm-lads clambered, trying to get hold of the large sausage at the top. People sang and danced to an accordion.

My relatives and I watched the hustle and bustle for some time, then sat down on boulders at the edge of the forest while the pale summer night rustled and breathed around us. We made a diverse group: the two girls and myself, then about twelve or thirteen years old, their elder brother from the cathedral college, and a young guest who was a Prussian junker in one of the smart Petersburg regiments. Then, of course, the lovely but temperamental governess Kaissa was also present. She flirted lightly with the junker whilst on her other side the college student, who was obviously infatuated with her, did not receive the slightest attention. For us girls, it all seemed 'silly', especially to me who was turning green with jealousy because the 'grown-up' schoolboy took no notice of me but had eyes only for the beautiful Kaissa. So we got up and wandered across a dew-covered clover field where we chased some young calves which should not have been grazing there.

When we returned to the edge of the forest, the others were no longer by themselves on the rocks; Karel sat towering between them. As usual, his furrowed face, weathered and as though chiselled out of stone, showed no expression but stared blankly into space. His peculiar clothing was slipping off and, noticing this, our elder brother jumped up and chased us away just as we had chased the cows. The breaking up was hasty, and for us the St John's night came to an abrupt end.

But behind us Karel's 'Ho-ho-ho!' resounded through the woods and over the village green while the dying embers smouldered.

Years later, Karel's life also smouldered to an end, a lonely, mysterious life, a surviving relic of primeval times. There are no longer any Karels today. Yet up there, in the north, the climate, landscape and the nature of the people made it possible to house those last sons of Anak,* belonging to a distant past.

8

Ivanisieva

The General was not a lovable father. His hate was so profound that it cut him off from the family like a shroud. He hated the Germans at the Tsar's court, he hated the victorious Japanese, and now he hated the revolutionaries who were turning St Petersburg upside down. His servant boy entered timidly when summoned. 'Your Excellency desires?'

'My daughter!'

Whereupon his daughter was soon in the room, simply dressed in white with a thick black braid which hung down her back. The green velvet curtains at the windows made her wide, pale face with heavy eyebrows meeting over her nose, appear paler.

'You sent for me, Papa?' she said in French.

'Yes, it is time that we talked a little about this impossible situation. Your dear Mama has already screamed enough and fussed about her clothes and jewellery, I can't speak with her. Sit down!'

Elizabeth sat down opposite him at the enormous writing desk.

She could not see the Tsar's picture behind her,

---

* The Old Testament founder of the race of giants, the Anakim.

but she knew that it showed Nikolai II with his wife and two eldest daughters happily together as a family. Elizabeth liked this picture in its white velvet frame. The reason why her father was always so angry and strict was simply because he wanted to protect these people. Oh, if only she could be a soldier, a general like her father! The Japanese would flee before her! The tattered rabble raging wildly outside would grow still when she rode among them on a high steed . . .

'Stop dreaming, Elizabeth. We must be quick and decisive — the catastrophe could take place today,' and her father explained how she, together with the servants Vanya and Ilka, should defend the house and her mother.

'Never be afraid of the masses, they are like a big angry dog which will cringe if you look at it sternly. You are big and brave — just do what our Tsar, our father, would want you to do. And above all, hate, hate our enemies, hate the common people, hate the betrayers.' A power like lightning shook the young Elizabeth to the depths of her being. All too soon, she became grown up and gained understanding. All too soon, the country's fate unrolled. Her father rode off.

There was fighting in the capital and the revolution was quashed, but her father was brought home dead, tattered and disfigured. And Elizabeth with her dreams of heroes? Her shrieking rang through the house; furiously deranged, she hit, scratched, bit and spat; hate, hate were her father's last words, now engraved on her heart as if by fire. For weeks she could only be held strapped to her bed. She recognized no-one and spat at her beautiful, elegant mother who stood by in despair. She would not eat, she would not sleep, she screamed and screamed.

Then, all of a sudden, there would be weeks of complete silence during which Elizabeth would rock the Tsar's picture in her arms, her hair wild, eyes vacant, her voice hoarse. She sat and rocked the picture. No other world existed any more.

Totally unexpectedly Elizabeth would once again be gripped by the demons of hate, and her screams, fury and lust for murder caused all to shudder. Only bonds could restrain her, her young body tied down with rope, the door locked and barred. The maids trembled, her mother fled to relatives, and the doctors discussed among themselves. The diagnosis was mental derangement, and the deranged had to be put in lunatic asylums.

When I saw her for the first time she was called Ivanisieva and had been in the clinic for a long time. There, they knew almost to the day the ebb and flow of her illness. If she was peaceful, they could occupy her by giving her the laboratory guinea pigs to take care of. No-one could have done it better. But when the dark times began, she would be racked with hate, giving in to the influence of terrible forces which spurred her on to destruction and murder. Her screams would ring out in the closed unit and her fists would thunder. Medication was not given in those days, protective care and cold baths were almost the only remedies. Again and again Ivanisieva returned to the hell of insanity.

Years went by. Ivanisieva's rhythm was upset by the First World War which must have penetrated through to her, releasing memories of her father, the Russian general, and remembrance of the fact that she was in a German institution. Indeed the rhythm of an illness can be upset and the best nurses are unable to observe when the dark times are unexpectedly approaching.

I was fifteen at the time and responsible for the hundred guinea pigs which the patients had to feed. I particularly liked Ivanisieva. Although the illness made her appear ugly and unkempt, it had not succeeded in dimming the bold light of her spirit. One day she came gloomily up to the guinea pig cages arranged upstairs and carried out her work in silence. She chopped turnips, distributed the oats and split wood for the little stove.

'What is the matter, Ivanisieva, you are so sad today?'

She looked at me with wild eyes, 'It is because you must die today. All Germans must die, it is the Tsar's command!' And she raised the hatchet.

'Oh, Ivanisieva, I see that you must kill me, but surely not here. What will the guinea pigs think? And haven't you heard that all executions take place out in the open, under God's heaven? Come, kill me in the garden.' Fanaticism and hate gleamed in her face. A fight up here would have meant no chance for me.

So we descended the stairs, I in front and Ivanisieva with the hatchet behind. 'Not one step too fast,' I told myself. I walked in front of her to the yard. There, the workers were standing and understood the signal I made with my eyes. It took three of them to tie her down and lead her off into the dark times which lasted longer than usual.

When in 1918 the War came to an end with a great famine, Ivanisieva's life also ended. Until then there had always been enough titbits to nourish her the way she had formerly been accustomed; now nobody had anything left. Many patients died of malnutrition, but Ivanisieva went before them all. As she lay in the chapel her face bore the soft glow of a sleeping child.

9

Aunt Puttchen

You have to imagine a large farm more than a hundred years ago. Puttchen, to her brothers and sisters was simply 'Puttchen' — plain daft! When her brothers rode out on their ponies and her sisters rolled colourful hoops along the garden paths in their lace dresses, Puttchen would simply stare with big eyes. When the tutor called his class together, she would obediently and quietly go along, dip her quill into the ink manufactured on the farm, and write 'Puttchen'. It never came to much more.

Nanny dressed and undressed Puttchen: that was what she was there for. She liked doing it because Puttchen was always friendly and patient. Everyone loved this child who never disturbed anyone or sought attention. When her sisters' dowries were put together with dozens of silly soft cambric blouses in bright colours, large lace collars made by the farm girls and boxes full of linen, a dowry for Puttchen was also laid aside, together with a bank account at her disposal. Nobody considered whether or not a

man would ever want Puttchen for a wife. Throughout all celebrations, Puttchen would sit there smiling
peacefully, at the hunts, at her sisters' weddings and
during the Christmas festival — always lovable and
daft. It never crossed anybody's mind that Puttchen
was not normal, so it was never noticed that Puttchen
was becoming an old maid.

Nanny dressed her in a tight corset over which a
silk blouse fitted closely, her broad feet peeped out
discreetly below the skirt hem, and her hair was
pinned up into a chignon. Thus dressed, she lived
many uneventful years. She was a friendly clock
which ticked away in the corner but did not show
the time. She continued to tick as the First World
War came and went.

Another boisterous generation grew up on the
estate, guests came and went, hunts took place, but
amidst all this Aunt Puttchen remained alone as a
piece of furniture is always alone. I can still see her
before me: her neat, round little form, a golden watch
chain on her full bosom, the small white hands lying
idle. And always those gentle dark eyes which understood nothing, yet gazed at one so trustingly.

We youngsters would curtsy, set out a chair for
her and bring lemonade. She was never without a
little purse at her waist in which there was a silver
box of chocolate biscuits. These she would offer us
with her soft shy smile, and, before the young crowd
had disappeared, she would walk with mincing steps
up to her room, to Nanny. It never occurred to us
that this woman's life was dazed or confused. There
was so much healthy strength to carry daft Aunt
Puttchen along through the years.

Her life became dramatic for the first time as it

drew to its close. The estate was expropriated, the property diminished, and Aunt Puttchen became ill. So she came to us in the doctor's house. The illness was diagnosed as serious: cancer of the lungs. As you entered the house from the veranda, the sickly-smelling vapour caused by the disease would hit you as it penetrated from above into every room.

Aunt Puttchen lay propped up by piles of cushions and remained unchanging, smiling and good. Only her hair turned grey and straggly in advance of death. Amongst all the medicines on her night table stood the little silver box, and we continued to accept the proffered chocolate biscuits, to thank her and then let them fall into the fireplace.

It was a grey, wet winter after the War when Aunt Puttchen passed away. She had not noticed that she was ill, or that her familiar world stood completely on its head. No-one would ever have allowed Aunt Puttchen to lack for anything. We all mourned deeply when the old clock stood still. But father, with his sense of style and humour, arranged for Aunt Puttchen to have the most special funeral ever. He loaded the small coffin on to a sleigh and drove alone through forest and blizzard until he reached the family graveyard. There, the pastor and he buried her. When he returned he said, 'Aunt Puttchen and I had a fine journey. The wind howled, and the sleigh tipped over a few times, but she was as peaceful and content as ever and we enjoyed a wonderful conversation about heaven and the good Lord.'

10

Jan

The hours in which Jan lay buried alive in a shell crater in Russia towards the end of the First World War were decisive for the rest of his life. Something happened to him, because from then on Jan was considered an idiot and could not really cope independently. Before they dug him out he still saw the small Lettish farm house and his little crooked mother who always called him 'my giant', saw the orderly fields and himself as he ploughed clean, straight furrows. Yes, he was even able to hear the cuckoo in the birches and the songs which the girls were practising for St John's Day. He heard himself calling out a good, manly joke to them. Then it grew utterly dark all around him.

Many months later while walking up and down the large ward he noticed that a long overall hung from his body. He also recognized white and blue stripes; he rubbed himself with his hand as if wondering, half asleep, what had become of his rough uniform. Another few months passed before he discovered that he was not alone; indeed, there were rows and rows of beds with colourfully hand-woven blankets on which men sat, all moving their mouths as if they were speaking, laughing and crying. Not a sound reached Jan. However, he took a broom in his hand and carefully swept together all sorts of crumbs and bits of paper from between the beds. An uncontrollable desire to smoke took hold of him. What could be easier, than to ask one of these men for a roll-up? That is what he thought he was doing, not knowing that his only articulation was a dull, bellowing sound like a dog barking with a muzzle on. No one paid any attention to him. An attendant entered wearing white trousers and a pink striped overall. Jan looked him in the face with questioning eyes. The attendant also moved his mouth, took the broom from Jan and slapped him good-naturedly on the back. Jan was happy. This man surely understood him, so he 'asked' again for a roll-up. Hergauk, the attendant, saw Jan's eyes. They were no longer clouded and dead-looking, as they had been for years.

At the director's next visit Hergauk had an important conversation with him. Jan was allowed outside: once again it was a broom which connected him to his surroundings. Now he swept a stable with yellow straw and hard, round horse dung; a good, worthwhile surrounding. The horses would come in from work and eat their midday oats, the stable boys would sit on the step smoking, and Jan would receive a roll-up.

What belonged to 'before' remained buried forever, no bridge led back to a name, home, or past. He grew accustomed to the signs people made and understood their commanding waves, their angry frowns, their joyous laughter. His love of order and cleanliness had not left him, even in this state of darkness, and his giant hands remained apt and nimble. Indeed, even a kind of vanity had survived, he only wore the dressing gown in the ward where everyone wore them. He was given a pair of trousers, high boots and a rough jacket, and he found a piece of mirror which he hid behind the hay-trough in the stable. He would go on errands for the stable boys, and he could smoke as much as he wanted.

Jan would have been a happy man, if only the dreadful, eternal silence had not enclosed him, if only they could have understood him. He 'talked' and 'talked', and they — they waved him away, friendly or rudely with the words 'be quiet, we can't understand you.'

One day my father came home at midday and said: 'I have a patient with me whom we call Jan. He was buried alive, has lost his memory, speech, hearing, papers and all. He seems to be a Lettish farmer boy and has been here for two years. You could take him along to the shore house, he works willingly, is clean and sensible.'

So Jan came to the house where our family lived during the summer. There were no houses or shops far and wide, but mile upon mile of sand dunes and woods, with the tossing, sighing sea a little way down from the house. Jan found excellent jobs to do. He chopped wood for the fire, washed dishes and saddled the horse for the youngest daughter. He picked berries, wove baskets, kept the whole house clean, and, in the little hut beside the horses, the cigarette ends piled up. He understood when his mistress showed him the cold hearth, and made a fire. He soon understood nearly every sign he was given. Most of all he liked doing what the youngest daughter asked of him. She was engaged and whenever her fiancé came Jan was there, ready to serve.

Then the first 'miracle' happened with Jan. The youngest daughter forgot that Jan could not hear anything and quite absent-mindedly she called out 'Jan'. Jan immediately turned round and came running. He himself remained quite unsuspecting, he had heard this voice so often within him that he did not notice the difference between within and without. However, when anyone else called he would not move an inch, and nothing penetrated through to him. From then on the youngest daughter could 'speak' with him. She would give him instructions in a soft voice — he would understand.

The second 'miracle' was that Jan, who was regularly given pocket money, bought himself a clock! Where, when and how nobody knows. He must have walked for hours to buy this clock. He spread out his savings before the youngest daughter and showed her that the big grandfather clock had cost the amount which was missing. Could he read the time, I wonder? He would often look at the clock face.

Then the third 'miracle': the youngest daughter was worried about her fiancé's absence. Had he gone swimming, or rowing? Was he in the woods? She shouted: 'Cari, Cari' and her voice must have contained a note of anxiety Suddenly there rang out from the top of the dunes a mighty bass voice: 'Cari, Cari.' Jan stood calling out to his young mistress' loved one, and therewith spoke the first word in his shattered life.

Everyone then believed that Jan might perhaps gain the power of speech again, but he stayed with this one word. Nevertheless, his inarticulated range of sounds could in time be considered a kind of language, with specific sounds always repeated for particular things. Whoever knew him could understand him.

Then the greatest 'miracle' took place: Jan sat in the kitchen, it was autumn and already dark and chilly. The youngest daughter had cycled twenty-five kilometres to the apartment in town and was expected back the next day. All of a sudden Jan sprang up making sounds of fear, crying out, 'Cari, Cari' and could not be restrained until he was allowed to go outside as he demanded. The giant returned hours later with the daughter, exhausted and in pain, in his arms. She had attempted the long journey back from the city after all, when her bicycle wheel had bumped against a jutting-out root, leaving her lying helpless with a pulled muscle in her foot, miles away from the shore house.

Shouting would have been useless, and crawling back through the dark likewise impossible; but she had called 'Jan,' quietly, the way she always did, and Jan had walked through the trackless forest in the dark to where she lay. The next day he also found her bicycle there.

For many years Jan lived at home until he moved with the youngest daughter and her husband to their small farm. The Revolution and the Land-Reform had completely changed life along the Baltic. People had to work alone, poverty had grown up, and the stony fields had to be worked with primitive tools. Here Jan developed extraordinary capacities; his enormous stature, natural strength, and his gaze which took in everything, were vital on the small steading. He could do simply everything; his young mistress only had to want something and his bear-like hands were ready for rough or delicate work alike. 'Machine broken!' — Jan helped. 'A basket for mushrooms!' Jan wove one. 'The children are waiting!' Jan was the most delightful child-minder. 'Shoes worn out!' Jan would resole them . . . There was no 'why' or 'wherefore'. He had attached his loyalty to the only person able to shine through his deaf and silent gloom.

Without showing surprise he went with the little family when, following the Nazi–Soviet pact, Hitler transferred all Germans from the Baltic lands to Poland. He remained the same in Poland, the factotum and friend of the two children. Nothing had changed for him.

Thus it continued until the Second World War was lost, Cari was imprisoned and the great flight began. It was experienced by thousands, retold by hundreds. Jan survived everything: the incredible marches alongside the youngest daughter's heavily burdened wagon, the ever decreasing number of household wagons as people and horses dropped out, fell behind, or separated, the chases whipped on by terror as waves of Russians gathered together behind the lines of fleeing refugees — and the loss of one of the children who was only found again six months later.

But Jan did not live to see the child again. The wave of Russians had rolled up and swept over the little family which, as if washed ashore, remained lying there, and only after a year found the strength and capacity to move on westwards. Jan was no longer with them. Shattered in World War I he had lived on for nearly thirty years, to be sucked under once again in the chaotic whirlpool of World War II.

Yet what a fulfilled life it had been, after his waking heart had heard the echo to its calling, and the ear of his spirit ear the sound of compassion through the dark cloak of illness which had robbed him of his past, his hearing, and his voice.

We still have one of Jan's little woven baskets discovered in the flotsam and jetsam of that time.

I I

Omichi

Since the story of Omichi took place Japan has changed to the same extent as Europe, and the mentally disabled have been included in modern progress.

We were able to follow at close hand a drama which, as if on stage, unfolded with classical simplicity. Yet it happened within my memory.

Omichi was born severely brain damaged and spent the first year of her life, from dawn until dusk, strapped to her sister's back. When the children played hopscotch on the street, as they do all over the world, her head jolted back and forth with each skip her sister took in her wooden sandals. Flies sat on her eyes and she was enveloped from head to foot in a warm dampness. Omichi cried when their mother took her out of the shawl which bound her firmly to her sister's back. It was cold and uncomfortable, lying naked on the raffia mat being washed and changed. Then her mother gave her the breast and rocked her, murmuring a little singsong and Omichi grew peaceful and let herself be carried around on her sister's back until the next mealtime.

Then followed years which can be counted by the

traditional dress: first the kimonos with large bright flowers for little girls, then the small flowered pattern for schoolgirls, and thereafter the sombre grey or brown, unimposing designs which adults wore. Add to this the straight fringe, covering the forehead like a lacquered black border, for children, later a braid for the school years. Finally, at twenty, the young women wore their hair soaked in oil and tied up into a knot over a rococo-style toupet. You could only sleep with the latter if you used a wooden pillow for support and lay motionless throughout the night.

Omichi learned all this, and she learned to eat her rice with black, green or red seaweed sauces, and her egg or fish with chop-sticks. She could not, however, carry her little brother on her back like her brothers and sisters. She also could not hold her drinking bowl delicately with her fingers in the correct position, and she could not go to school like all the other children in the village. School means life. In Japan children love school just as birds love flying. Up and down, all movements, all happiness, all the twittering has its source in the school. Through finely drawn brush-strokes painting the increasingly difficult signs across the paper year after year, the world entered the school in pictures, in stories.

Only Omichi sat on the step of her parents' house, first small and colourful, finally big and dark. She sat idle, eyes crossed, looking angry, while her hands snatched like swift dogs whenever an unsuspecting person approached too close to the little witch who would rip their kimonos from their backs. The brothers and sisters avoided her as they avoided the red centipedes which crept into the house through the swing doors to bite them. Their mother took care of her and suffered. What would become of her?

One day the mother put on her best white stockings and her good sandals, and pulled a black silk kimono over three other kimonos, then neatly folded. She placed some provisions for a journey and tied her purse into a furushki — a blue kerchief with embroidered gold birds on it, which she had received on her wedding day. She drove to the big city. She found the clinic and bowed deeply to the doorkeeper many times before venturing to ask him whom she should turn to. The door-keeper also bowed and guided her to the ward nurse who in turn showed her where she could bring Omichi to be looked after for the rest of her miserable life.

That evening she arrived back at the village. Bowing before her husband, she asked him to come out to the front of the house where no-one could hear them beneath the thick bamboo twigs. 'Father, I cannot take Omichi there,' she said. 'There are many, many Omichis, and all of them are so angry and sad, just as she is. They are all in cages like our cricket hanging on the wall which only sings in the evening. They are like the little bear which Chokichi San, the merchant, keeps behind a grid so that it doesn't bite the children. I can't lock Omichi behind bars and go away saying she is well off. That isn't true. I can't do it, father.'

'But what shall we do with Omichi?' said her husband. 'We certainly can't keep her here. Just think of the other children. We have already let them suffer far too long under Omichi.'

Mothers all over the world are the same. They nearly always hold on longest to the weakest and most sickly child. They still see in the deranged son or daughter the spark of love and life, of longing and of light which lies so deeply buried. Omichi's mother was no different. She now knew the lot awaiting Omichi when she, her mother, would no longer be there.

One day the mother said goodbye to the family before going on a 'beautiful journey' with Omichi. Laughing and waving they all stood in front of the little house. Holding Omichi by the hand, the mother turned round once more, and bowed low, smiling at them all. Then her wooden sandals clattered away to the railway station.

They travelled to the foot of the Asama Yama, a high volcano. Both locals and tourists climb to its glowing crater at night, to stare down into the raging red throat of the mountain. The ascent is very strenuous and long. On the lower slopes bloom rhododendrons and azaleas, gigantic butterflies fly into the small bamboo woods without scraping their wings. It smells of fruit and the hot sun on the stony path. Omichi let herself be pulled forwards without looking about. But her mother saw everything. She saw how the bushes fell behind and the slopes became more barren, she saw how the jagged rocks of lava increasingly covered the mountain side.

Year in year out, a stream of people are attracted to climb this sinister mountain livid with fire. Among these are foreigners with their hired guides carrying garlands of straw sandals round their necks, ready to rebind them under the ladies' and gentlemen's shoes. For, after many tired and thirsty hours of walking, everyone, including we Europeans, reaches the ash-region where sharp black pieces of volcanic ash cut the soles of straw sandals to shreds and, layered ever higher and deeper, make every step a torment. We belonged to the foreigners, of course, but Ama-san, the honoured maid-servant, had come with us and, with her confiding chatter in pidgin-English, made the strenuous walk lighter and shorter.

Omichi and her mother had overtaken us like all the other Japanese in their high wooden shoes. They held on to the ever larger volcanic rocks as they pulled their feet out of the ash, step by step. Suddenly Omichi sat down, and stubbornly made it clear that she did not want to go any further. Her mother took some fruit out of the bundle and so enticed her daughter on. In this way they finally arrived with the last climbers at the top.

The crater was so large and so full of steam and smoke that one could not see the other bank. Everyone was silent with awe before the thundering swirl and hiss, the bellowing and whispering which blazed out of the colourful depths. A boisterous young American wanted to drop a tin can down into the chaos. Someone grabbed his arm: 'Stop, don't! that's dangerous for all of us! Everything you throw in, the Asama Yama hurls out again, together with lava, ash, fire and boulders which would shatter all of us here.'

A little aside, the mother squatted down next to Omichi who was tired and moody. Did she see everything there before her, woven into the smoke which rose up in regular thrusts, her little house, her thin, overworked husband with his wrinkled neck, the children in blankets sleeping huddled together with their father in the soft glow of the round ash-stove?

She dozed a little; the foreigners rested and ate appetizingly sandwiches which their hotels had prepared for them. Ama-san spread our provisions on to a cloth which soon became warm from the lava stones. Omichi slept soundly and thereby did not attract the attention of her compatriots. For us and the other tourists the difference was unnoticeable; destiny weaves close and concealed. Everyone watched the colourful clouds of smoke, and the roaring, seething steam. All were silent, as one should be silent before the great mountain gods.

Finally we all set off in order to be half-way down the mountain where it was lush, green and blossoming, when the sun rose to cast his early splendour in tenderest colours. Only the mother remained sitting, holding Omichi's hand. When the quiet, polite Japanese, the foreigners with their guides, and we too, all indifferent and unaffected, were already quite far, the mother got up and, taking Omichi by the hand, walked straight into the glowing crater . . .

Suicide in the Asama Yama was a common form of death at that time, we were told later by Ama-san. Love sickness, illness or despair drove people to the mountain which was reliable and final.

Walking below we saw for a moment a pillar of fire rise out of the Asama Yama, and heard the thundering roar of erupting power. Then it was still again at the top. No one spared a thought that two women who had shared the tiring climb up, did not share the return journey back to life. If Ama-san had not been with us we would never have learned what happened, how it began, and how it had ended for Omichi, who was 'different'.

12

Travelling Companions

In 1918 our family was stranded in Japan. There was revolution in Russia, the Tsar had been murdered, and civil war had broken out. One lived from rumour to rumour. Somehow we would have to get across the gigantic, burning country to reach the Baltic states at the other side. Hardly had it got about that the family wanted to attempt the journey, when other travelling companions appeared: we were asked, 'in God's name,' to take along two mentally disturbed people. I, at seventeen years of age, was asked if I would take on the responsibility of their care, to which I enthusiastically replied, 'Yes.' Without a clue I took over the work of an adult for the twelve-day journey. The journey, however, was to last eighty-eight days.

When we went aboard the ship in Japan — Father, Mother, four children, the cook Tio, and thirty pieces of luggage — Marusya and Mrs Halla were already on board. Marusya was fifteen, fat, with cheeky eyes and curly blonde hair; Mrs Halla was weak, slim, and elegant. They were being watched over and held firmly; both were so ill that they could not be left alone for a minute. I went into a cabin with them and we were locked in from the outside. Through the peep hole I watched the Japanese harbour, with all its commotion, disappear. I also saw the Korean city of Pusan as it appeared on the horizon. We then lay down in the comfortable first class sleeping compartment and looked forward to rolling from East to West throughout an uninterrupted journey.

Everything turned out differently. We were all arrested and held captive for twenty-four hours in an inn in Seoul: the family, the cook Tio, two mentally disturbed patients and thirty suitcases. I tried to get to know my charges. Marusya (a nymphomaniac) had to be washed and combed, Mrs Halla wept and looked at herself in her little hand mirror. Marusya, fascinated by the Koreans with their pointed hats and long shirts, continually made signs to them. Mrs Halla took no notice of anyone or anything. They both tried to escape several times daily.

When the journey finally continued, the last connecting train in Harbin had left. For seven weeks our family was held up in Manchuria, the heart of the revolutionary fighting, while a general of the White Army stopped the Nikolai train to Russia, and the Bolsheviks blocked the Amur line. The railway station was crammed with thousands of people, stranded goods wagons and locomotives. With the help of children and the cook Father managed to commandeer a small second class wagon, from where it lay in deep mud between the tracks. An ideal dwelling, with even a closed-off compartment for me and my patients. As the lock was broken my father fastened the door shut on the outside with a rope. Every night the carriage would be shunted on to another line, while the locomotive's tuneful whistle, which the children called 'Polka Harbinka,' rang out shrilly. With the carriage came Wong Fu, a

Chinaman as shy as he was lice-ridden. We had to make the compartment window opaque with soap in order to prevent Marusya from luring in any men who were standing about. Mrs Halla looked in her mirror and allowed herself to be spoon fed.

On the very first day Father found work: at the Harbin Hospital he had to step in for the head doctor who had had an accident. Americans, from an aid train on the opposite track, came daily to learn Russian from Mother. The cook would take Wong Fu and the children off into the over-crowded city to search for food. Cooking was done on a small primus stove, clothes were washed in the toilet. For a small tip the 'composer' of the 'Polka Harbinka' would drive to a side track and fetch oily, but hot water for the water tank. I washed, fed, and took care of my patients; sometimes they were lethargic, sometimes noisy and lively. In the evening they would pull off their shoes and hit me with them.

At first all this was very interesting, but as life in the train stretched on into weeks it became unbearably tiresome for all concerned. We longed for deliverance, but how?

Then a fellow-countryman appeared and set everything in motion. He had been an officer and the Reds were searching for him. He wanted to risk making the rest of the journey to the Baltic as a civilian and member of our family. We had to try and connect our carriage to an eastward-travelling train and then to join the Amur train in Khaborovsk, thus avoiding the fighting of the Reds and Whites at the Front. It may be that the two deranged women acted as guardian angels, because we succeeded with a great deal of cunning and bribery in hitching the little wagon on to the end of a long train so that it was pulled, hopping and shaking itself like a dachshund, through Manchuria. Wong Fu would sit de-lousing himself on the steps where the children and Tio the cook also liked to sit, singing in rhythm with the wheels.

Now the journey had really begun. At night the great spirits of the East crouched on the roof and howled: during the day one could experience one's own forlornness, as the train of sixty carriages shrank to a thin metal rope winding its way through a vast, mysterious wilderness. During the night the two 'departed from reason' (as the Russians say), would be gripped by a demon-like restlessness. Marusya would pack, bundle up and fuss with her luggage, whereas Mrs Halla would swing in a gentle, weight-less motion in and out of her bed like a billowing veil. Their voices complemented each other to create an eerie, uninterrupted tragi-comic whispered duet which rose and fell like the tidal blowing of the taiga outside. I tried in vain to comprehend it.

The rift caused by the severing of the Tsar's king-dom reached as far as the eastern rivers, forests and mountains; it splintered right up to those regions where the spirit of the nation suffered, where the bewildered guardian saints were no longer able to help, and the first echo vibrated in the sensitive mem-branes of those with disturbed souls. The 'normal' people held on to their crazy illusions: it will pass; fight and hold on till the end. The 'crazy', however, threw themselves into the chaos of doom.

During the day everything was brighter and easier to manage. The exhausted patients liked to sleep and the children would come to the compartment with playing cards to relieve me for a few hours. It was

Mother who held the travelling household together. The two men were inwardly preparing themselves for the border crossing. Despite the revolution they were gentlemen, there was no doubt about it.

In Khabarovsk at the Manchurian–Russian border they were both immediately taken captive, while a large crowd of Bolshevists searched the carriage. On the neighbouring track stood a train with hungry, miserable prisoners of war in a goods wagon, waiting to be transported home to Germany. The children secretly handed out pieces of luggage to the prisoners through the toilet window, where many willing hands took hold of the bundles and piled them things up between the tracks. They also told us that there was an empty saloon coach standing somewhere round the back. This was helpful because now we had to leave Wong Fu and his wagon, since the cursed bourgeoisie were no longer permitted to travel in their 'own' vehicles.

Of all the customs left over from the Tsar's time it was bribery which survived the longest. The saloon carriage had in fact two attendants, plus the silver samovar which belonged to it. For an appropriate sum paid daily, they were prepared to take on the family. They sat, one at each end of the blue luxury coach, weeping 'because the axle was broken,' while the thirty pieces of luggage were hastily transferred over their heads. The patients, before whom even the commissar shrank back, came last, while the cook with the two youngest and Mother moved into the new home within a few minutes. This amazing accomplishment was wholly the result of Mother's admirable presence of mind. The head commissar had a splitting headache: she gave him a tablet. He

tried to open a Japanese security box with his bay-
onet: she showed him the lock and the harmless con-
tents of lady's handwork. She was so calm, organized
and polite, that the whole crowd left without causing
any damage.

In the midst of the alarm and frightening search
she had also remembered to post the children at all
the important points and to send the two eldest to
look for the men. My sister and I ran like mad from
one station shed to another. A locked wagon — were
they in there? A railway worker replied: 'These here
have been locked up for days, condemned to death.
They will be taken away today.' In such instances
one does not pause to reflect or ask questions but, like
an artist under the spotlight, lives only to fulfil one's
task. Finally we opened the door of an isolated shed on
the loading platform. We saw our father and his friend
standing against the wall, guarded by many armed
men with their backs to the door and we saw my
father's wink as he pressed his lips together.

Well before the border, a joyful rumour had com-
forted some of the refugees: namely, that a Swedish
saint, Elsa Brandström, was, like all true saints, to
be found wherever help was needed. So the small
cardboard sign 'Swedish Mission' had caught our eye
during the breathless search. Hardly able to speak we
tore open the door: before us was a bare room, a
table, and a friendly Swedish couple from the aid
group called the 'Brandström Charity'.

Within a few minutes everything was under con-
trol; the 'harmless Germans from the Baltic' (the
friend's uniform had been thrown out of the toilet
window just in time) were freed and led in triumph
to 'the wagon with the broken axle'.

As the last bell for departure rang out Mother said: 'And this will be repeated at every station!' For heaven's sake, no: and off I was sent to the commissar with the headache to beg for a certificate, a *bumaga*. I owe it to the involvement and experience with my patients that I got it; I remained calm as the second stroke of the bell sounded, and continued to wait calmly as the man finally tore a corner off a sheet of paper and scribbled down that he had already performed a thorough search: his comrades may allow the family to pass on. To this day Mother has kept this life-saving scrap of paper. Oh, good old, careless Siberia of those bygone days! When I came running up without a stamp on the paper my father sent me straight back again. The commissar had gone, but a friendly militiaman stamped it. At the third bell all hands pulled me up the steps into the blue wagon. From now on this was to be our home.

The Amur is a wild and powerful river; its torrents roared down past the train. The desolation all around was so boundless, that one can only compare the journey to a trip by air, where nothing but sky stretches in all directions down to the horizon. Forests, hills, wilderness, forests, wilderness, hills, day and night always the same, except that the cold increased, until the last spring warmth of the ocean turned into Siberian winter. The last carriage of the train was occupied by prisoners of war returning home, and now and then their songs would resound. Otherwise everyone was as if enveloped in sleep, especially myself who should have been awake. The family's blue wagon was superb, with cupboards, chairs and a table, proper sleeping compartments, and a small lounge. My sister took over for me in the 'loony bin', as they called it. I immediately fell asleep. There was a tearing screech of brakes, whistles and shouts.

The prisoners had seen someone jump from a carriage up front and had pulled the emergency alarm. Mrs Halla had disappeared! Like a shadow she had slipped away from the children who had been playing cards. Father jumped out into the frighteningly deep snow, and, as the train driver would not wait, Mother threw down a fur coat, blankets and warm clothes from the moving train. Before Mother could prevent her, my sister jumped down after them. The last thing the family saw was Father running, a bundle of fur, and a fifteen-year-old child on the tracks. In the train the début of a would-be nurse lay shattered.

In the next town we managed, with lots of money and shouting, to have our carriage disconnected. How much more suitable it would have been for the new dictators simply to have turned out these bourgeois on to the streets, and to have kept their luxury coach for themselves. Yet in those days an unquestioned authority of status — successfully stifled and under attack though it was — still existed. One still dared to order and bribe, even in the name of the saints (although they had been invalidated too!) One was obeyed. Our Baltic friends made telephone calls down the line. A trolley was sent out, and after hours of torment Father and my sister arrived, but there was no trace of our patient, not even a footprint in the snow, nothing.

So the Brandström Charity was called out again. This time it was a 'blue lady'; her hat, high boots, and muffler were all made out of bright blue velvet. The blue lady was very efficient, soon arranging for me to have a tiny room in a wooden house. I was obliged and had to stay until my protégé was found, over four thousand miles from St Petersburg! I was seventeen years old and had always led a very sheltered life. However, Duty was always written with a capital letter in our family, and it never entered my head to shirk mine.

Our carriage was blocking the line and the officials urged us to connect it to the next train. At that time trains were still running daily to the West. Meanwhile, the search continued. Though there was only one telephone for the railway line word soon got round on the 'grapevine'. Large reward! Large reward! Lunatic escaped! It was surprising how quickly the news travelled to every corner of the taiga. The next day officials began to threaten us, the carriage had to go. The family now faced a final decision: either lose their mobile home and thereby the possibility of travelling further, or to leave a child behind in Siberia.

Again it was the mentally ill who came to our aid; a myth had been preserved about them from the time of the Tsar: those who were 'lost to reason' were subject to mysterious, heavenly forces and therefore protected and helped by every Russian soul. Because of this the family was allowed to stay. On the fourth day a little track inspector arrived on a rail trolley with Mrs Halla. Dishevelled, coughing, with frozen toes and her veil sleeves billowing she said slyly, 'I was only joking!'

13

Ilyushka

Ilyushka's life was connected to our family by invisible threads. Three times destiny knocked him down and tangled his life's path into an unrecognizable confusion. Hardly back on his feet again, he would find himself under the protective shadow of our family. He was born by the Volga, on a large estate by the steppes. Three nations and three religions looked into his cradle. Firstly, the Protestant German estate owners who were our uncle, our grandmother, and the manager. Secondly, the Russian-Orthodox household: servants, maids, coachmen, and amongst them were Ilyushka's parents, Ivan and Manya, who were second coachman and washerwoman. Finally came the hundred or so Muslim Tartars who were estate workers living in a kind of enclosure within the yard.

Father Anatoli was the only one left over from the earlier Russian estate owners, and this old priest and his chapel were hardly used. The few other Orthodox Russians came to Mass on Sundays and to confession at Easter. What could old Father Anatoli do all day long on the endless plains of the steppe? All his love and energy were dedicated to the only Russian child, Ilyushka. Manya the washerwoman felt honoured; she would never have been able to make it possible for her small son to learn even the alphabet, if it had not been for Batyushka (little Father). Ilya, however, studied the learned church liturgy, and at the age of five could read the Gospels and holy apostle stories like a little deacon. Father Anatoli gave him still more; he diverted him from his mother's apron strings and the fear of his father's horse whip. Ilyushka realized — and not a day too soon — that there was only one refuge for him: heaven and the all-merciful God living there.

Our Grandmother seemed to be related to this God. Every day Ilyushka had to bring her eggs from the hen-house. He was already uneasy as the hen-woman pulled his ears so that he would not let any eggs fall. Then Grandmother would take him to task: 'Only a hundred and fifty duck eggs today! Run and find out what is the matter!' He then took hours to deliver all the eggs. There was no reward, but he would be permitted to watch the owners' children from afar as they rode on their steppe ponies, or in the evening sang to their aunt's guitar, whilst gigantic frogs croaked a bass accompaniment from a neighbouring pond.

It was hard being sent out by his mother on to the steppe to collect camel dung when she needed some to heat her washing kettle, because that was the Tartar youths' privilege. These heathens' sons would beat him up, unless he managed to escape beforehand to his father's stable. The fifty coach and riding-horses were good Orthodox Russians: the Orlov and troika trotters, and big Kukla for the genteel lady's saddle. No Tartar boy entered here.

The most difficult yet most desirable of all tasks was that of driving out with the master: the dog-cart with a black trotter racing across the steppe, the master and his shotgun taking up the whole seat, the dog between his knees. Ilyushka sat squeezed in at the side. Then suddenly his master stopped, and Ilyushka bashed his head against the rail. He was supposed to be holding the reins: quite calm, quite relaxed, so that his master could hold large field glasses to his eyes and stare out across the shimmering steppe, across the grass which rose and fell in the wind like waves. The head of a prairie hen was visible, the dog jumped from the wagon and his master grabbed the shotgun, saying: 'Keep on heading for the ravine!' Both horse and dog knew that their job was to chase the prairie hen to the edge of the deep gorge so that it would be forced to turn and run against their master's shotgun. Ilyushka trembled as he held the reins of the black giant, envisioning in his mind's eye how in their exuberance they would all rush headlong into the ravine, to be dashed to pieces. Then he knew why Batyushka Anatoli had taught him the long prayer for help in moments of great danger.

The following year brought with it the greatest need for that prayer, but Ilyushka could not say it because the need concerned his own head, and his own head knew nothing any more: an infection of the brain, as hopeless and final as these things were seventy years ago. Despite all signs to the contrary he continued to live, although an '*imbécile*', as Grandmother would say in French at table so that none of the servants could understand.

Manya had given birth to a little Misha just as the sickness began. The master and mistress helped a great deal, but since there was no free medical care or social service Ilyushka remained a burden which

Manya and her husband could not carry. They had to separate. Manya took the children and travelled far north in order to be wet nurse to our Russian relatives. The second chapter in Ilyushka's life began.

He was not aware of the singing on the Volga paddle steamers, he hardly noticed the endless waiting on the many railway stations where Manya would crouch between her bundles on the platform and give Mishka her breast. He laughed, friendly and idiotic, when a passing railway workman pulled off his little fur cap and threw it somewhere out of reach: 'Fetch it, then!' He drank the tea his mother prepared in the kettle which dangled from the bundle. Dreamily he chewed his bread with his back teeth — the front ones had fallen out without his realizing. 'Seven years old and already like a little deacon,' his mother would tell her fellow passengers who would look at the dumb round face and shake their heads in disbelieving sympathy.

The last stage of the journey was the quickest. A troika drove them from the station to the farm where Manya was to nourish the master's child; such a milk receptacle had to be nobly transported. Then, when Manya was dressed for the part, something like a remembrance of Father Anatoli, his golden vestments, the church candles and vessels glimmered in Ilyushka's eyes. Manya wore a snow-white, richly embroidered blouse with short puffed sleeves of lace, and wide, rustling skirts, pink because the baby was a girl. Framing Manya's face like a bright crown of pearls was a bonnet which hid her hair, with long pink and white ribbons fluttering down her back like flags. Round her neck hung five, six, on some days ten strings of softly shining glass beads the size of hazel-nuts which were supposed to occupy and delight the child. When Manya took the baby on her arm and unbuttoned her blouse at the front then it meant: 'Out you go, lad!' Ilya would obey his mother and go into the wet nurse's room to his little brother. There he put a cloth dummy, soaked in pre-chewed bread, vodka and sugar, into the only too hungry mouth so that he would be 'good' and not disturb the illustrious amah.

When the ladies and gentlemen were sitting at the tea table Manya would carry in her small mistress to show all the uncles and aunts the rosy, healthily smiling baby. Ilyushka would stand shyly in the doorway: the samovar shone like pure gold. Before being refilled each empty glass teacup was washed by the young mother in a little brass bowl and dried with a long lace cloth on which hens or woodcutters were embroidered in red and white. Crystal bowls filled with *varénye* (boiled fruit), and shiny silver cake baskets were passed around: 'Uncle, dear, some more? Aunty, dear, would you like some of this?' Everything was enveloped in the steam from the samovar. Was Mass celebrated here? Ilyushka frowned and tried with all his might to remember. 'Lord have mercy, Lord have mercy,' went round and round in his head.

He saw the icons which lead their own life in the right corner, protected by the ever-burning light; there is the Virgin, Mary of Vladimir, the *Otrada i Otlushénie* (comfort and joy), and the baby Jesus with his hand on his mother's mouth. There is He, the Pantocrator, there ride Boris and Gleb in the their glorious robes on their palfreys — where had he seen them before? Where else did such proud steeds exist?

But his embellished mother was already rustling from the room with the pink baby. 'You've a nanny worth her weight in gold, Verotshka; genuine peasant stock from the steppe. Your baby will flourish with her!' Ilyushka heard the aunts saying as he followed his mother out.

The years went by. Of Ilyushka there remained only a shadow of his former self, his true being had crept beneath the bear-skin under the dark cover of disease. He grew to be a youth and yet was still a child, and a child he would always remain.

Then the war broke out in 1914. It was hardly felt on the estate; there was always enough to eat and the only change was a lack of horses and the men who had been called up. Manya had long since stopped breast-feeding, yet she lived only for the child whom she served night and day. Her own little Misha had died.

Ilyushka was ordered around good-naturedly: 'Put on the samovar. Saddle the pony for the children. Fetch salad from the gardener. Open the door for the visitor . . .' No-one bothered about him, no-one even considered putting him into an institution. Those enshrouded by darkness are holy, whoever is 'lost to reason' finds the reasons of the whole world at his disposal: we will serve you.

Now and then recruits marched past the estate, the right bootlegs decorated with a tuft of hay, the left with straw. The command 'Hay — straw, hay — straw' from the sergeant's mouth kept them in step. 'Hay — straw!' cheered Ilyushka in quick reply, hay — straw: a very clear command. He can do it, he can repeat it! And he simply walked along with the next company which marched past on the country road. The soldiers were also Russians; they accepted the simpleton as a mascot and let him march with them.

Thus began the third radical change in Ilyushka's life. Naïvely and without an inkling as to what it was about, he experienced everything the soldiers went through: marches, battles, hunger, cut feet, enemies, coups, revolution, civil war, and again, shooting, plundering, shouting and once more hunger, thirst and cut feet. Small, with a round child-ish head and dark button-like eyes he ran along, no weapon in his hands and an old, over-long army coat flapping against his legs. 'Duck!' they shouted and he ducked. 'Run!' and he ran. 'Drink, Brother!' — and he drank. He often drank too much, but he survived four years without being wounded. Then the splendid firework display about him disintegrated to a heap of ashes. His comrades fled in all directions of the wind, while new rulers chased, captured and shot them. These new rulers at the Baltic Sea were the 'Germanzy,' the German soldiers. They were upright, precise, and had good doctors. It was not long before they diagnosed Ilyushka as an 'idiot' and he was delivered to Seewald in an ambulance.

The third phase in Ilyushka's life rounded itself to the first. Here was the right place for him to retrieve and meet his inner self. Was that not the same master of the Volga and steppe again? And Ilyushka asked my father: 'Who are you, sir?' The samovar gleamed golden on the table when Ilya entered the room; was it not how it used to be when Manya and he went in to say good night?

Despite the diagnosis Ilyushka was not put into the closed unit. My father gave him a room in the coach house and employed him in the stables, so that he could receive some little pay. Then it was discovered that Ilyushka was in the habit of drinking one too many, and he was scolded because it was not allowed. This reminded him of grandmother and the eggs! Ilyushka's past shone ever brighter though the rubble heaped about his soul.

Then at last a day in November came when he went to the city for the first time. He blackened his boots, pulled on his long army coat and the coach-man's old peaked cap. It was very late when he returned, but being the child he was, he still came into our sitting room to say good-night. 'You are drunk,' said my father. But Ilyushka winked and replied: 'Sir, you mustn't scold me, God has granted you a great favour through me. I was in the church, in the cathedral with the five domes, and have taken some consecrated bread for you and the mistress.' So saying he pulled a small piece of consecrated bread from out of his army coat and offered it to my parents on the palm of his hand.

Since that day his life continued peacefully. He had his simple chores, his stubborn ways, drank occasionally and was chided. Nearly every day he visited his golden church two miles away, marching with arms swinging like a soldier, his wobbly legs doing what they wanted even when he was quite sober. Nearly everything he did was wrong, and yet he was agreeable to everyone because one and all loved this child of God. He would go through fire for his master, yet still threatened him with his finger: 'Sir, sir, you mustn't scold me because then God will withdraw His grace from you!' At Easter he kissed all of us with the three Easter kisses; on Christmas

Eve he came solemnly to receive his gifts. It never occured to him that he had been given an exceptional position: he was home at last.

I was in Berlin when my mother wrote that I should try, amongst the many Russian immigrants, to get hold of a Russian Bible for Ilyushka. That was his greatest desire. When I returned for my next vacation I brought with me the very Bible for him: fat, heavy, with a lock and embossed with gold. We invited him. He had shaved and even put on a collar, his face was deeply serious. My mother held out the Holy Book to him with both hands, but he knelt before her, crossed himself, kissed the Bible, and finally even my mother's sleeves. Then he took the precious possession in his arms, his clumsy feet gliding smoothly he left the room like a high priest, and his emotion so transparent that the tears came to my eyes.

The following morning the whole family was sitting talking together at breakfast. The door opened and in came the 'little deacon' beaming all over his face. 'Ma'am, I can read the Bible, and last night I was reading and there it was, plain for all to see, yes, it's written clearly: "Drink, but do not get drunk"!'*

We do not know any more what has become of him, but we hope that the Russians have remained as we knew them in that those 'departed from reason' continue to be recognized as brothers in need of their brotherly care.

* Sirach 31:28f.

14

Mère de Beauregard

We were travelling by tourist class to South America. One makes friends easily aboard ship, and very soon different social groupings had formed; together they enjoyed board games, the concerts on deck, or dancing in the evening. Every morning the enormous saloon which held several hundred people was full of broken bottles, papers, empty cigarette boxes and over flowing ashtrays. The stewards would only clean up after morning Mass was over. In the meantime they hung about the swing doors, making comments about the various congregations which set up their travelling altars in five different places and then quickly and quietly celebrated, while the few believers, mostly old women, knelt like pious little islands amidst the rubbish left over from the pleasures of the night before.

Quite a large number of clergy were on board as well as an ancient nun who was travelling to a convent in Chile or Peru with four young, pretty novices who looked out anxiously from under their enormous wimples. The abbess reminded me of an old bird who fed and watched over her not yet fully fledged young ones. After all, they were being forced to live amidst the hurly-burly of carefree passengers. The cabins of their class had no portholes and were very, very narrow, while outside the sea wind would

71

tear at their billowing, flapping habits. Therefore they chose to sit right at the back of the saloon, furthest from the bar, where they would whisper together or pray. In their devoted silence they stood out, and were again and again the object of both approving and malicious glances.

Later, when everything was over, I was briefly told the story of the Mère de Beauregard. She was at that time seventy-six and had gone into a convent at sixteen. For sixty years she had not left the walls of her ancient abbey. The French passenger who told me this also maintained that she had wanted to return to the world again during the first years, but the vow had been taken, and her sacred duty held her captive. Now with her protégées she was travelling for the first time, with an important task and tremendous responsibility. She was completely defenceless in an indescribably alien world.

We had been six days out at sea when it happened. The sunlight sparkling on the sea had taken on an increasingly southern character, dolphins and flying fish accompanied the ship, and hungry seagulls screamed continuously overhead. The calm weather had enticed us all on deck, to promenade arm in arm, to laugh and talk. We were all under the spell of the tingling new air, Europe had sunk far behind, and we imagined long-forgotten pirates emerging as we sailed through the Caribbean Sea, past the Bahamas and the Greater and Lesser Antilles.

All at once we saw the venerable Mère de Beauregard flapping towards us along the deck like a great blackbird. 'Stop the ship, stop the ship, I want to get off!' we heard her cry in despair. We all gathered round the old lady, who neither saw nor heard, but had 'taken leave of her senses' in the truest meaning of the expression.

The captain hurried out and tried his best with his seaman's humour: 'Please, Madam, do step out, but it is rather wet around here.' No one laughed, it was too obvious that something was very wrong. The person before us was no longer herself, even her features were unrecognizable, yet there was no doubt that, as the only nun on board, it was she, but she was not herself. The four young girls held hands, trembling. An elderly Dominican Father went up to them with an air of authority and asked them to enter a cabin with him and the Mother Superior.

We all stood around waiting. There was hardly any dancing or noise that evening. One of the stewardesses, a pretty Italian, spread the news that the old lady had had a dream and was out of herself on that account.

We all heard about the dream. The ship would sink, it would run against a reef, burst open, and sink. And Mère de Beauregard, who had spent sixty years bound to duty and obedience, did not want to sink with it. She wanted to get off, she wanted to be saved, and neither the Father nor the novices' tears could shake her out of this delusion which had so unexpectedly entrapped her. So it was decided that the next day she would be sent to the nearest harbour on the Bermudas. From there she could travel with our ship's sister steamer which would meet us at our own destination within an hour of our arrival.

The move took place without fuss or delay. All the passengers went ashore, where they were dazzled by the unbelievable array of colour of the fruit, flowers, fish, streets, trees and people. No-one

troubled about Mère de Beauregard. The lonely little
novices remained in their corner, even more shy and
inconspicuous, while the Dominican watched over
them like an old sheep-dog who had now taken on
his master's duties.

The next evening, already far out at sea, a film
was being shown. We sat in the ship's cinema staring
at the wobbly pictures with English subtitles. Suddenly the light went on, the film stopped and the
loud speaker announced: 'A radio message has been
received. Our sister-ship has just run aground on
a rock and has a leak. Nobody injured.' The film
continued, but no one paid any attention to it. The
announcement became the focal point, and confusion
broke out. 'So the old nun's dream was right, now
she's walked straight into disaster, got on the wrong
ship — oh, what luck, otherwise our ship would
have hit a rock.' and so on. For three days announce-
ments came every few hours: The leak had been
repaired, they just had to wait for the spring tide
now, which is expected tomorrow. No, it was only
due in three days; the passengers had been shipped
off the reef; the ship would be unloaded. Even
humour came across: they were sitting on the rocks
drinking Scotch.

The spring tide came on the fourth day, and the
next announcement was that they were on their way
to Europe. Everything on board is in order.

So we journeyed on and forgot. For most of us it
had just been a diversion. But whenever I think of
that trip, Mère de Beauregard appears in my mind,
thrown out of herself by the force of a dream; a
desperate little shell which tried to save itself and lost
the way.

15

Frau Scheuerlein's Death

This episode occurred in Berlin during the time of inflation and hunger. I was training to be a nurse and was on night duty. The patients had received visitors, and the bedside tables were laden with jars of soup, parcels of cold meats or cakes and, of course, flowers, which I now carried out for the night. The large ward was dimly lit. A hoarse voice, trying to whisper, called to me. I went over to the bed which was separated off from the others by a screen: 'Yes, Frau Scheuerlein?'

'Go on, Nita, don't leave me alone when I'm dying, will you?' She begged, using the informal '*Du*'. A forbidden and unheard-of conversation. Never were patient and nurse allowed to address one another thus, and particularly not to discuss the patient's condition! She had come from Bavaria to the capital and ran a public house here. As is so often the case, she had taken to drink. The result was dipsomania, heart failure, and a painful death in this large ward.

However, this woman's great soul was unable to die. Her spirit wandered restlessly about in its last dwelling place, forever searching, searching. After a few days I was discovered, a person who understood her. Young as I was, I was affected by her spirit the way a seismograph is affected by an earthquake. So

75

when the attacks came and she would clasp me tightly round my neck, screaming in torment and fear, I knew, far beyond the calling of my profession, that my task was to sympathize and bear with her.

The night drew to an end. The day nurses told me that Frau Scheuerlein's relatives had come again during the visiting hour, checking that her dentures were still in the glass by her bed. The nurses were not to forget that they belonged to them, when Frau Scheuerlein finally died. No notice had been taken of the person passing away in front of their eyes. The dentures; they mattered.

I went to the matron to hand in the night report. 'It's just about over for Frau Scheuerlein,' she said. I gave a start; as night nurse, I was supposed to sleep now, according to official regulations, but to let Frau Scheuerlein die alone was impossible.

Instead of going to my room I slipped behind the screen where she lay. There I stood thinking back over the months we had known each other, of the priceless moments of joy when the true Scheuerlein had shone through, full of humour, ridicule and hoarse laughter, of the sparkling black eyes when the illness held its breath and allowed old mountain wisdom, vivid portrayals of drunkards, children, friends and enemies to flow forth. I thought of the terrifying hours of maniacal raving and animal-like screams of terror which had reminded me of a trapped lion, of the disappearance of any expression whatsoever, when a medical examination began, the matron took her pulse, or her relatives came to inspect. Then Frau Scheuerlein could play death and listen with eyes closed and indifferent mien to all that was said about the old boozer.

I now looked down at the yellow face, the burning eyes, the fine nose with nostrils vibrating for want of air, and heard the whisper: 'You'll stay, won't you?' Yes, I stayed.

'Sister Nita, your night duty is over. Please leave the ward.'

'But I would very much like to stay with Frau Scheuerlein.'

'That's out of the question, where would it lead to? Now, please!'

I went to my room, tidied myself up and in half an hour I was back on the ward. My heart skipped a beat when I saw that Frau Scheuerlein's bed was gone. Already over? The other patients followed me with their eyes; it was a mystery to them why Sister Nita showed so much concern for the only 'lunatic'. I, however, heard and saw nothing until I found Frau Scheuerlein in the death-chamber, a large, bare room with glass walls and three high arched windows. Truly a 'store room' for that which was superfluous in this organized institution.

'Scheuerlein, how's it going?'

'Pretty rough; oh, dear God, Nita, stay here until it's over.'

And I placed myself beside the dear, disturbed being, held her wasted hand and waited. Her breathing grew increasingly laboured. The matron came to give her an injection and energetically sent me from the room, absolutely furious at such a lack of discipline, Hardly was she gone than I was at the bed again. Frau Scheuerlein now lay quite still. Only her breathing rattled in an ever faster rhythm, to slow down again until it had almost stopped, before building up to another crescendo. Tightly her fingers gripped my warm young hand which was not allowed to release them, and at intervals between the rattling of her breathing came the question: 'Nita, you there?'

However, nothing must upset the discipline which, once set in motion, could not bear any human extravagance. Matron returned again. This time she locked the door behind me and took the key away. The window! I went through the garden around the house, everything was in full blossom, and the hot sun was dancing on the bushes . . . The three windows of the death-chamber were wide open, but they were well out of reach and there was no way up. There was only my voice. 'Scheuerlein, are you there?'

'Aye, Nita, so long's you're here . . .'

Ten minutes later: 'Scheuerlein?'

'Aye, Nita.' Again and again.

And then a last gasp, 'Nit . . .'

When I again intruded the day nurses were in the process of laying out Frau Scheuerlein. 'Quick, Sister Nita, you liked her so much, help us, we won't say a word!' Thus I was allowed to wrap a white bandage round the now peacefully sleeping face, thereby closing her mouth, and also to fill in the pink death certificate attached to Frau Scheuerlein's right foot, with name, date, and number, according to the regulations.

16

Hanni, or the 'Imitator'

The revolution of November 1918 broke all bonds. The German army hurried back home from the Baltic. In one of the railway carriages stuffed full with soldiers, horses and baggage, sat a girl beside a young corporal. She was following him out of a rich, spoiled life into an unknown world.

The young man travelled back to his home in South Germany, married the girl, finished his studies, and was ready to face life. But his young wife, 'transplanted' to this foreign soil, groped tentatively through the years and never really felt at home.

This couple had a child with Down's syndrome and hoped, through cures, extra education and strict discipline, to make the child 'normal'. With endless, painstaking effort she learned to read, write, and carry out household tasks. Her happy, optimistic nature brought great light into a marriage which suffered under the parents' opposing natures.

I met Hanni for the first time when her father was fighting in the Second World War. The Nazi doctrine of 'life not fit to live' resulted in the annihilation of such children. The mother was ordered to hand over her daughter, and in desperation she came to me: 'Save my child!' Only a bold move would be of use here. So I went to the head doctor of a famous psychiatric clinic, introduced myself as the daughter of a colleague, and asked him to write a testimonial to the effect that Hanni was capable of completing a year in household management. I needed her for my own five children. The professor respected my trust in him and wrote the testimonial. Hanni moved in with us.

Hanni is difficult to describe: her crooked back, small rib-cage beneath the short neck, her forehead and slanting eyes, her dribbling, open mouth with its thick tongue hanging out, the jerky, scarcely formed speech, her difficulty with breathing and, above all, the clumsiness! Yet all this is forgotten when you experience her complete lack of guile and her positive acceptance of everything at all times.

At that time our family was also being swiped at by the Nazi paw with arrests, the banning of our work, and other restrictions. We also experienced the well-known fact, that the talents in a community only develop under pressure. The first step was to leave the city for a place in the backwoods remote enough to hide us. There our sixth child was born, and some of the other children were able to attend the village school. We lived close to farmers, but needed space and an income: numerous children, who were being hidden from the régime or the bombs, found their way to us, among them Hanni.

When we had expanded to nineteen people we had to think about building, in the middle of the war! It was thanks to the remoteness of the area that we succeeded in erecting a real house without fear of controls, despite having only obtained a permit to build temporary accommodation. Silent and staring, Hanni worked with us through every phase: she saw how I reported the completion of the roof while we were really only laying the foundation. She experienced how this foundation was built up by small children, a seventy-year-old bricklayer and ourselves. She was with us when in the dark of night we all made a chain to unload cement and stones brought to us by a brave woman in a truck. Hanni witnessed how we continually bartered, using our ration cards as a basis and living on wild fruit instead, until all the materials were gathered. She learned that ceaseless work could keep one's head above water.

She took in everything gladly in her ungainly and clumsy way and was never disheartened. Typical of her condition every job 'stuck with her'. We were all hard pressed and Hanni could not be spared, her 'training' year turned into many years. Hanni's father fell at the front; the war ended. At last she was allowed to return to her mother, to the village where everyone knew and liked her.

In the meantime Hanni's mother had become very delicate while the little daughter returned grown up and changed. Before the war, Hanni had kept her parents' pedantically clean house in order, now she returned like a soldier, the experience of a pioneer in her back-pack. Darning socks was no longer worth mentioning, greater things were now important! So while her mother, confined to bed by her fragile health, struggled on in growing despair with the daily routine, Hanni hatched out her plan.

First of all she looked for work: she delivered newspapers from four to six in the morning, cleaned at an inn from six to nine, cared for an old man from ten to twelve, and was once again busy at the inn until late afternoon, only returning home towards evening. Then began the misery of arithmetic; the newspaper accounts never balanced! Numbers did not belong to Hanni's world. When she was told, however, that she was to inherit a many-figured sum, she knew spontaneously what the money would be good for. Building!

From then on she followed a familiar, trodden path. She imitated step by step our secret building during the war, succeeding even in times of peace in keeping it a secret. Bank statement clutched in her hand, she found an architect sympathetic towards her curious project.

When the plot of ground was bought and the foundations laid, she went to the mayor to ask, 'Am I allowed to build?'

'Certainly, yes Hanni, you may do that.'

'Then please give it to me in writing,' and, smiling, he wrote it out: Hanni had permission to build.

When the pretty little house with a balcony and small garden was finished, Hanni hired a cab and told her mother to come with her. Where? To our new house!

There they lived many happy years together. Hanni's fire for working has not died; even now, after her mother has been buried for many years, winter or summer she rises at the first grey of dawn, as we had to do during the war. She suffers from varicose veins and a heart complaint, but she will not give in! She celebrates every festival as we do, with candles in her house, candles in her soul. When any dignitaries of the village meet her, they doff their hats in greeting. In Hanni a strength manifested which many healthy people could not imagine.

17

The Eagle

The home for orphans in the Bulgarian city was full, which is why Konzos, the night-watchman, felt annoyed when he heard the soft whimpering outside the door. Konzos and 'the nurse', skinny Duna, cared for the children, ran the home, cleaned the place, in short did everything — and full meant full! However, as soon as it was light and the streets filled with people, for better or for worse, Konzos was obliged to fetch in the latest addition. Wrapped in newspaper lay a scrawny baby boy, his head twisted to the left, hands hanging limp and the tiny wrinkled feet blue with cold. On one corner of the newspaper written in large letters was the name: Nikóla.

The foundling babies in the home lay opposite each other on two long planks with cracked brown sheets of rubber beneath them, and old grey soldiers' blankets from World War I covering them. Duna passed around a few beer bottles filled with warmed buffalo milk and water, with the same old worn-out teats. The older and more clever babies would hold tight to the bottle-neck, the smallest and weakest would let go: no records were kept; was it weeks or months that such a little body needed before starving to death?

Nikóla was fortunate with his bent neck; nourishment flowed into his mouth without much guidance.

He did not scream like most of them and because he did not kick much he did not become dirty from the filth which flowed down the brown rubber. When he could walk 'nurse' put him out on the street: there had been very few coins slipped into his paper bundle, too few to support him any longer.

Nikóla was still more lucky: not only was his neck squint, but his little brain was 'squint' too. He nevertheless had the appetite of a wild dog, the timidity of a cat, and the simple guilelessness of young sparrows which cannot count to three; all this left him to grow up like a small animal in the dust. Apart from this, there was absolutely nothing which could tempt anyone to kick him or throw a stone when he slipped past the door sniffing hungrily.

Much later it became apparent that a great strength dwelt within this creature — a strength of longing, of searching, and the memory of a bygone Light. It was later recognizable that he had been continually waiting for something. When he felt that he had caught a glimpse of that Light, Warmth and Greatness for which he searched, his face would light up with a smile which even the most modern people had to call 'heavenly'. We believe that such moments were rare. Perhaps at dusk, when he lay huddled in his rags against a fence, and the majestic Vitosa Mountain peak suddenly arose out of the haze to reach up and touch the heavens. Or when he was woken at midnight by the deep drum-beat of the gypsies in their camp, drumda-drumda-drumda, drawing him into the rhythm so that he felt part of one giant heart.

One day he wandered into the zoological gardens where only the king was allowed to stroll about. The

soldiers had not noticed the little grey creature, while
he slipped past all the cages without looking at the
animals; they were nothing new or special to him,
just wild and lonely fellow-creatures like himself.
But when he came to the bear-pit with gravel spread
evenly on the ground and saw the young king holding a conversation with a bear, Nikóla smiled again.
The bear knew his master well. He rocked to and
fro with joy and contentment, while the king fed
him through the bars with nuts which the bear took
first between pouted lips, then held in his paw,
making funny little noises of pleasure. The king
nodded and swayed back and forth like the bear,
laughing like someone for whom laughter had
become a luxury. What a pity that he did not see the
shining face behind him in the bushes, or notice
Nikóla as he crept out backwards past the attendants
into the noisy city.

All day long Nikóla wandered about the stalls in
the indoor market. Higher and higher, right up into
the vault each stall was richly laden with all kinds of
wares: rows of green, yellow and red pepper-pod
necklaces; mountains of green and blue cabbages;
pyramids of purple aubergines. Here were water buffalo calves in their brown skins hanging in a row
from their hind legs, blood dripping from their cut
throats to the plaster. There were the round wooden
trays laden with pots of yoghurt, men walking
around selling drinking water from gleaming brass
water-cans with long spouts, or little boys dragging
flat baskets of dried black plums. Nikóla saw all this
with the hungry and thirsty eyes of someone who is
never satisfied. Here there was no cause to unfold
the wondrous light which lay hidden within his

heart. No one was prepared to give anything away; hunger decided his fate.

He went to the street where he slept. There the grand villas had well-fenced gardens which gave him shelter during the night. From here he could see out over the poor peoples' huts to the hazy mist in which Vitosa Mountain stood enveloped.

At the corner stood an old tree, around which the 'General' had piled water melons. The General had fled from Russia and lived by selling water melons. He slept beside them, wrapped in a long coat with his fur hat pulled down over his ears. Today he was still awake because a foreign lady was haggling with him over a water melon: 'That one's too big, the other too soft, this one isn't even ripe, and all are too expensive!' Finally she found the right one, but there was no boy at hand to carry it for her. Nikóla had been watching from his sleeping place, the General saw him and shouted: 'Nikóla, come here a minute, and carry the lady's melon for her.' Immediately Nikóla's heavenly smile welled up from the depths of his soul, transfiguring his eyes, his mouth, his filthy hair and his bent neck. He loved the General; when the latter spoke Nikóla felt light and warmth, and his hunger vanished. The lady saw this smile, and although she was a hard, embittered person, his smile reached a depth in her inherent in every human being, in which lay buried a seed of longing. She simply kept Nikóla with her after he had carried the melon home.

We know very little about that time. We only know that they travelled together like mother and son through one country after another, experiencing many situations, but neither of them experiencing

86

the sunlike smile again. Nikóla was brain-damaged, and he 'knew' this with the dreamy wisdom common to the abnormal. The smile was the reflection of warmth and light which entered somewhere into his sunny being. The window to his inner being was as small and narrow as a crack in a wall; only determination or rare coincidence could reach through. The lady, however, had merely noticed that he was retarded. Doctors and teachers were called in for advice, psychiatrists admonished and warned. But the lady allowed unwarranted cures and therapies to wash over him, gymnastics, medicines and hygienes; all kinds of teachers, tailors, orthopaedists. Nothing but drill, drill. Not a bit of heaven, not even the size of a handkerchief.

Indeed, Nikóla did learn reading, writing and arithmetic, and in the course of the school year he produced remarkably varied things — childish scribbles and nonsense beside essays which were almost too advanced. Complete failure in arithmetic would be followed by a good knowledge of history spontaneously, bubbling out as if he had invented it.

When Nikóla was twelve years old the lady, then resident in Germany, brought him to us. We were told that he had to learn discipline, that he was lazy, rude, and deceitful, that he was capable of everything, understood everything, but refused to comply. He simply would not recognize what had been done for him, or admit that he owed anybody anything, and so on, and on, and on . . .

Nikóla, his head hanging sideways and his long arms limp, listened. He remained with us unhesitatingly. We found a suitable school which was not too far by train, and he went every day with two other boys. As always, his reports showed ability ranging from very good to very bad. He took no notice of anybody, and looked at us as if at strangers who were not worth getting to know.

Once, on the way back from school, he was standing with his friends in the last compartment of the train. Suddenly, he threw his cap on to the track, and stared after it as if expecting it to jump up and follow him. At the next station he got out and followed the line back to where his cap was lying. It was very late when he returned home with his cap on. For the first time I saw his smile. It was unforgettable!

Nikóla stayed with us for about two years; reserved, passive, always watching slightly mockingly to see how we would react to various things. The children loved him, but he never took up contact with them. We always encouraged artistic activities, such as music, painting and modelling. Nikóla just looked on. Months later he suddenly took some clay in his hands and modelled a bird: a perched eagle. Sometimes one sees such an eagle in the zoo, wings laid back, the sharp head erect, looking into the distance; a personification of loneliness and submission to fate. Nikóla had never modelled before, now he produced a small work of art.

I took it to the workshop to be fired, and Nikóla waited eagerly to see if his eagle would return again undamaged from the tremendous heat about which he had been told. When he held the masterpiece in his hand again a few days later, his face lit up with a smile, his radiant smile which can only be described as heavenly. It was as if the eagle had released it by greeting Nikóla, coming to him as a brother, like the bear had come to the young king. Slowly and gradually Nikóla made himself at home with us. Then his rash, impatient 'mother' reclaimed her boy, taking him back to her flat where she tried her own methods to increase discipline, to shape Nikóla's development. One can never tell where ambition, disappointment, and domination will lead.

Nikóla reacted in his way. He locked himself in. For four days he remained in his room; nobody tried to coax him out, no-one spoke a kind word through the keyhole. After four days the lady's patience wore out and she had the door broken in: but Nikóla had already been dead for four days. His head rested on the table beside the eagle, a razor blade beside them both. Beneath Nikóla's chair his crusted blood formed a pool. His long arms hung down limply, as they had done thirteen years before, when an old newspaper had been his only covering.

18

Meli

It was in 1960. She was brought to us when she was eight years old. With her and her mother came a little brother of four years who very conscientiously watched over his sister. Her medical report was filled with all manner of diagnosese, but the authorities concerned had given up any prognosis — a day-school for brain-damaged children would at least relieve the strain on the mother.

Our chauffeur and the helpers carried her in so she could not thrash about, but she could scream enough to take your breath away. They sat Meli on my lap and, as if indifferent to her, I had already begun to sing. I sang a Russian cradle song which endlessly repeats the same phrase, the same rhythm, the same warbling melody. Meli continued to scream for a long time, but eventually the soft rocking and singing soothed her, so that she grew quiet and lay limp in my arms. From that first day until she left two-and-a-half years later, that song was almost the only means of checking her screaming fits and calming her down. The foreign language, as well as the rhythm and tone, all this anchored her personality which was disintegrating in screams. When glad and relieved, she resembled a flower with its head to one side, a beautiful and complete being.

When I saw her again many years later, still more ill and disturbed, she spontaneously intoned her cradle song; she had forgotten nothing.

Meli was a lovely child, with white-blond hair framing a delicate face, surprised blue eyes forever wakeful and rarely closed, even at night; she almost never slept deeply. For me her appearance was like a protest against her world.

I got to know her world. Her father had been sick with tuberculosis for many years. Two children were born, one during and the other after the war. Both became infected with brain fever. Even with strepto-mycin brought in by the occupying American forces, the eldest child could not be saved. He became epileptic, deaf and dumb, and died in a psychiatric clinic.

The cure only took effect on the second child, who thrived. Then Meli was born, and the brain inflammation soon became apparent. The poverty in the house was severe, but some social help was given. It was not possible to carry out a cure with Meli. She would smash all the furniture, and the mother had been extremely mistrustful of cures since the death of her eldest child.

This is where the riddle begins. There was a pause of four years, then once again a baby boy was born, two years later another child, and then again. I had warned both parents beforehand.

'But the priest said . . .' remained the one unshakable argument. The two youngest sons again did not thrive. The sickness had gripped the family, destroying their lives, their happiness, their future. The mother, so terribly over-burdened, suffered 'turns', could not sleep at night, but scrubbed, polished and cleaned, until the consequences of this enormous and demanding taboo eventually broke her.

Of all the important experiences in my profession, Meli's fate moved me most deeply. The dulling and extinguishing of a lovely little rose. 'What happened? Where has she gone?'

19

The 'Communist'

When I went to the interview for the post of director in a home, Gero was already there. He sat dumbly in a corner, indifferent to the noise and games of the other small patients, as if he were alone. 'There's nothing you can do with him,' I was told. 'He's daft, deaf, and dumb.'

The home was poorly furnished, the therapeutic possibilities minimal, and the conditions unclear. I did not feel exactly enthusiastic about the job. Then I felt Gero's gaze upon me from beneath his overlong eyelashes. A look from one human being to another, alert, questioning, slightly challenging even. His look pierced me where I am most vulnerable, in my innermost centre, where the insane find their home. I took the job.

After one year Gero was 'socially adjusted'; he was quick, keen even to grasp the educational activities. Apart from the uncomfortable but understandable tendency to remain alone, there were no difficulties. If only he would speak! Not one sound crossed his lips. His mother, whom we met every day at the bus, would say: 'If he could only say Mama, or not even that, but just a sound, one syllable! How many doctors I've tracked down, how much trouble we've been to, all in vain.'

There were also many Down's syndrome children

in the home, these mischievous little rascals. One of them, our Peter, was having a 'naughty day' again, and would not lie still. In order that the co-workers could have a rest I gladly looked after the children during their midday sleep. Like a spider I sat in the middle of the dimly lit room, with the beds in semi-circles around me, the ever wakeful Meli, who was afraid of lying down, sitting on my lap, and Gero's bed closest to me. Again and again Peter got up, instead of obediently lying under the covers, and immediately, as if swayed like stalks by the same gust of wind, thirty-five children sat up to see what was the matter.

Down's syndrome children do not let themselves be ordered about, so I decided to give Peter a little shock to make him lie still. I had read in a report from an English home that incomprehensible words like 'abracadabra' would amaze these children and distract them from their stubbornness. So I said to Peter: 'You are a *spe-cia-list* at getting up!' Peter froze, he pulled the covers up to his eyes, and all the other children did the same; had Illeberg — as the children called me — pronounced a terrible swear-word?

At the same time Gero, who since his birth had appeared deaf and dumb, who had not even gurgled baby sounds, sat up. His friend Peter had been insulted! With his beautiful eyes he glared at me and shouted: 'And you, Communist!'

My reaction was a burst of laughter; relieved that Gero could speak, amused by his warlike attitude and amazed at the word which I presume he had heard at home on television. All the children joined in laughing, it turned into a delightful afternoon, and the small troop even did me the favour of lying as still as mice and resting.

At the daily meeting I told the co-workers that they should try to build on this first impulsive word, and in a few months Gero's patient kindergarten teacher did indeed succeed in teaching him childish speech. His mother came to us in tears of happiness after he had said 'Mama' for the first time. We only tried to avoid reminding him of his first laughing success.

A few months later we received one of the frequent official visits: a mayor and his large retinue from another city which wanted to build a similar day Home. We led him, the officials, doctors and educationalists through the whole establishment, and finally into Gero's room as well. The great man greeted all the children and then offered Gero his hand: 'What's your name, my boy?'

Gero raised his long eyelashes, looked at the strange man and said: 'Gero Bumhardt,' and after a pause, 'Communist!'

O Gero! Your first word, your first triumph! Once again you wanted to be the centre of attention. The sixteen ladies and gentlemen broke into laughter, unnecessarily loud. I stammered and tried to explain this unusual greeting, but my guest was in a hurry to leave.

Only a journalist remained behind, and I asked him: 'Tell me, was it necessary to laugh so hard at the little boy?'

He replied: 'Yes, madame, that was well planned. You know of course that this gentleman leans to the extreme left in politics!'

20

Rosa In Lima

The old flower lady closed her stall for the day. She carried her basket filled with gladiolas, roses, lilies and countless unknown flowers to a corner of the garden. We gringos had given her permission to store the flowers here overnight. The glorious mass of blossom richly decorated our garden, and it was a help to the old woman. She stole the hearts of our whole family, but so gradually that we hardly noticed it. Suddenly the bent little figure with her wrinkled face and straggly grey hair was indispensable to our life in this foreign country. The old woman came early to fetch her basket, and laughed. In the evening she came, tired and dusty, often with nearly all her wares unsold — and laughed. She laughed whole-heartedly, a happy, contented laugh; indeed, we Europeans thought that such a woman had no worries, and we almost envied her existence with the flowers.

Today when selling was over, the little flower lady sat down on the lawn, in the shade of the wall and said: 'I can rest a little, because Rosa is dead, nobody is waiting for me.'

'Who is Rosa?' one of us asked.

Then we were told the truth about something which had often half-consciously moved us gringos like a creepy ghost story.

Again and again as we passed in the car, we had seen one or other coal-black creature crouching by the road beside fruit carts, in front of church doors, half hidden by thorn bushes, or leaning against an old wall. Once one of these figures had thrown off her black cloth, ripped it up into little pieces and then sprang about naked, a horrifying creature with matted hair, screaming and raving.

Another time we had seen how a similarly wretched person slipped off a low wall in his sleep, so that his feet jutted out on to the road. A car driven by locals ran over his legs, swerved, and then sped on. We had difficulty catching up with the vehicle and compelling the driver to take the injured person to hospital. We realized that he was astonished by our suggestion. The victim was still lying on the road as if nothing had happened and the driver was asserting it had nothing to do with him.

Now, listening to the flower lady's story, it became clear to us that all these black figures, usually motionless but sometimes frenzied, were all 'lunatics', the mentally disturbed who no longer belonged to human society. Shadows in a world of shadows, in no man's land. They were only nourished by waste from fruit stalls and rubbish dumps, the sky was their roof, the road was their bed.

The flower lady had given birth to a daughter on the name-day of St Rosa of Lima, when great processions were marching through the country; the city was filled with music and celebrating crowds. No-one came to help her, only a neighbour was there to hold a blanket across the open side of the hut which consisted of woven mat walls. Behind this Rosa was born. It was not easy because the baby had a head like a large melon; never again would it be easy with this sick child.

The mother carried the child strapped to her back to and from the flower stall, not for just one year, but for four long years, because Rosa refused to learn to walk. Neither would she speak, or even grow properly, which in a way was fortunate because otherwise it would have been extremely hard to carry her *and* the large flower basket. Eventually Rosa learned to crawl a little, so the flower lady left her at home in the narrow alley, while she went out to sell her flowers. Rosa could not get lost there, as the mat huts were joined together in a row and the place was teeming with big and small children.

In this way Rosa learned early to be on her own, if she noticed it at all. She had been 'daring' enough to enter the world on the day of a great saint, and that was why she was being 'punished'. She had been given everything: mouth, ears, eyes, hands and feet, but God had not given her the power of reason, and without it how could she learn to walk, speak, sing and laugh? Indeed, she could not even recognize something, not the other children, nor the old cat 'Chicita', nor the doll which she had been given by a neighbour. She lived, and that was all.

'Yes, gringa,' said the old flower lady, 'that's how it is, you see, until you've paid penance for the sin. She died yesterday, after sitting over forty years up there on the big road where the wealthy drive for entertainment or to go swimming. Three times I bought her a new piece of black cloth, and not once during all these years have I been able to buy something new for myself. My Rosa had it better than the other "black shirts", because every evening I

97

would bring her a wooden bowl filled with food, and she had a good position, since she was always thrown a few *soles* from the cars which drove past. She's better off now though, because now she has her reason back and is allowed to recognize the saints and sing with the angels.'

21

Nine Profiles

I often try to imagine what it would be like to have a mentally retarded child. It is true that I grew to love some of my small patients so much that I well nigh made them to be my own. But is that not theoretical? Can I, a mother of eight healthy children, really place myself in the position of a less fortunate mother? Here are a few different lives.

Karin

A child is expected. Everything is prepared, knitted, sewn, painted, made. And in the middle of the special hour which brings the height of expectation, the mother is suddenly gripped by a fearful horror: it is not her child wrestling its way to life. She is shaken with repulsion and opposition as if to a strange, irresistible enemy. She does not want to see the newly-born child; the doctor is faced with a problem. The baby has all its limbs and shows every sign of being a healthy child. The mother is spared all contact with her baby, and as yet no one notices that the little girl has Down's syndrome.

When I first met Karen she was two years old and her mother had never held her. The behaviour of the mother was a riddle because such a child is almost never rejected by the parents; the clumsy charm of these children nearly always wins over every heart. Now two valuable years had gone by and the symptoms of anonymous, unloving hospitalization had left their mark. I am sure that she never lacked adequate physical care, but who, in these clinical times, had enough homely warmth and kindness with which to envelop such a child? For the lack of these qualities no one is more easily disappointed than a Down's child. Whatever might have been developed, whatever trust might have been planted in this child, has been submerged under hygiene and daily routine. Now one can understand why little Karin has become so estranged that her mother continues to reject her; today? Tomorrow? Who knows, until the end of her life?

Delia

How different it is for Delia, a Down's syndrome child born into the world after seven brothers and sisters. She is the perfect example of what I would describe as the of a Down's task child in life: to sow and to reap love. Unimaginable poverty pervades the home; the family live in a make-believe world, have no settled abode, and all they own are the clothes they stand up in. When we fetch Delia to go to the day school every morning her seven brothers and sisters are with her. Trousers ripped at the knees, jackets from charity donations which — I wonder why — are always so long and baggy that the children have to hitch up the shapeless sleeves before doing anything. Their shoes are three sizes too big or non-existent. They all have runny noses and indescribable hair. Their mother, careworn and anxious, lifts the little girl into the bus. She is dressed like a respectable city child, with all sorts of ribbons and frills to make her look still prettier. The whole family pet and caress her; it is not easy, waving good-bye to the light of their lives for an eight-hour separation.

But the mother had heard that such children must learn early in order to succeed in life, and that is why she came and enrolled her child with us. 'But if anything happens to our Delia, we'll come with a hundred neighbours and bash you up with sticks!' What a promise! Under this 'dire threat', the little princess of the slums flourished enormously with us. Then in the evening when she returns to her home which has cardboard instead of glass for windows, where the children sleep three in a bed under sacking and rags, is the utter poverty irradiates with joy over the reunion. And as we drive off we notice one of the little brothers queue at the coal cast with a few pennies for three lumbs of coal.

Sanna

Sanna was an eight-year-old Down's syndrome girl who travelled all the way from her home in a distant suburb by car every day, in order to learn 'writing' with me. We painted large 'E's, and 'U's, and beautiful suns, clouds and stars in our book. Sanna was very polished and neat, like a shiny little apple.

Breathless with enthusiasm she would unpack her satchel and tie on her apron.

'Come on now, we have to learn,' she would call out each time when everything was ready.

Her vocabulary was not very extensive, but what she learned stuck fast in her little head. She had the typical memory of her condition, and that is why I tell this story.

A friend of our family was being treated by a throat specialist nearby. As she lived at the other end of the city she would sometimes come and rest after her treatment, before returning home. I would say: 'Sanna, we must be very quiet now, the lady is tired and wants to sleep.'

So we would whisper, which Sanna enjoyed tremendously, her head bent close to mine over our book, keeping 'very quiet'.

Later I took over the directorship of a home in another city. Years went by and I heard nothing more of Sanna. Our friend, however, was once walking along the street seven years after her throat treatment, when she passed a woman leading a of Down's syndrome appearance girl by the arm. The girl stopped, ran up to our friend beaming, and shouted: 'Lady tired?'

Ella

When Ella was of school age her mother brought her to be enrolled. The school doctor looked at her curiously: 'Have you ever noticed anything unusual about the little girl?'

'No. That is, she is a bit cheeky, and she can't articulate clearly, but you see, she has often been ill — pneumonia three times, an infection of the throat four times, and she nearly always has a cold. Also, some foods don't agree with her; but she is so sweet and loving, and we do everything we can think of to keep her healthy.'

Then came the school check-up and the diagnosis: Ella has Down's syndrome.

She was sent from the first school but accepted the following year at a school for difficult children. However she was once again rejected and the next year went to a special school which also soon informed the parents that it was impossible for Ella to take part in classes. She came to us at the day home. It was always a special joy for us to educate children like Ella. With tenderness and thought her mother had encouraged whatever development was possible for her. Ella was clean, could dress and undress herself alone, ate with good manners and, above all, her trust in the world around her had never been disturbed. One could build on this foundation.

Her destiny is a typical one for most of our Down's children. Sensible parents who could see that to be illiterate was not a disgrace, who helped us to give their children an active life by showing patience, and rejoicing with us over each piece of work, every song or play mastered by the child; such parents came to us through our Down's syndrome children. Once they had overcome the initial shock, especially when the condition was recognized as late as with Ella, these parents formed a reliable guild. We heard the same every day at the bus stop: Ella, Dora, Peter and John can already clean shoes, fetch milk, dust, and stand at the window waiting for daddy at the right time. 'They can do everything, absolutely everything — why should they learn to read and write as well?'

Ilsa

I experienced one tragic exception: Ilsa. Her father in his despair did exactly what a child with Down's syndrome can least cope with; he despised, praised, punished, mocked and threatened her, with the result that Ilsa became his very image. Despite everything, her mother made a desperate attempt to bring her child to a day centre. At thirteen years of age Ilsa swore like a trooper and swept everything off our office desk with her feet, since her mother was holding her hands. Flowers, telephone, files and pens whizzed to the floor.

I asked the mother to let her go, and in an instant she ripped out a handful of hair from a co-workers head. Then she pounced on me, grabbed my hair and climbed up me like a monkey to kick me in the face. I took her wrists and calmly flipped her to the ground in a somersault, after which she jumped up at me again. We repeated this little circus-act three times before she stood still in front of me, eyes rolling and her fists clenched.

I clapped my hands and called out: 'Come on, Ilsa, again, we're not finished yet!'

But Ilsa had had enough. She sat down on the sofa and listened, while her mother and I talked. Unexpectedly I felt a hand laid softly on my cheek, and heard her whisper: 'Ilsa good.'

As you can imagine, I wanted to take Ilsa on, but a bureaucratic veto against this problematic case made it impossible. We then heard that in consequence the father first attempted suicide, then pestered the authorities and newspapers for years with his troubles. Could one blame him?

Eo

Eo had also 'learned' from his choleric father. His special weapons were the little chairs for children, which he would deftly hurl out of the window or at us. Eo was small and delicate. He allowed himself to be diverted and soon afterwards even to be occupied in the nicest way. In the workroom he would make small bird-houses and folders, and eventually he could even write 'EO' on the blackboard.

And so after a few constructive talks, his father realized how much depended on his own attitude in preventing restlessness and aggression in his little son. Soon Eo's father and mother also belonged to the invisible guild of caring parents of Down's syndrome children.

Elli

Unfortunately, one sometimes sees teachers making mistakes. A teacher told me the following story. His special school was in the same building as a normal high school, whose headmaster competed a little with the headmaster of the special school. It is so easy for a school teacher of normal children to consider the curative teacher as a lesser specimen of his own kind.

There was a girl in the special school with a tendency to Down's syndrome who could go to and from school alone. One day when she was on her way she felt an urgent call of nature, and disappeared quickly

104

behind some bushes surrounding a neighbouring church.

Unfortunately, the high school headmaster saw this, and felt obliged to speak at once with his colleagues of the special school: 'And this is how your children behave!'

The headmaster called the curative teacher over and asked him to speak to the child himself, so that such little accidents would not be repeated in the future. Trying not to frighten the little girl, the curative teacher said carefully: 'Look, Elli, you could easily have held on until you were home. People just don't do that. Apart from that, someone saw you, and he must now think that you are a very badly brought up little girl.'

To which Elli replied: 'But no, Teacher, that can't be so. I certainly couldn't have any longer held on. But I shut my eyes very, very tightly.'

Ah, if only that headmaster had done the same . . .

Richard

It is hard when a healthy, flourishing child is attacked by meningitis and one is suddenly faced with a deformed and unknown stranger. Not a trace remains of the lovable baby-talk, the sweet gestures or unhampered steps. Stumbling, hopping, or only-walking-on-tiptoes sets in, he cannot hold a toy or a spoon, but babbles agitatedly, eyes staring blankly; oh, the changes possessing the child are so many, once one of the centres of that miraculous apparatus, the brain, is infected.

Richard's parents were completely bewildered by this phenomenon. Outwardly harmonious good looks remained, but one could not tell that it was the same child. They took him to several hospitals and finally to a university clinic of high reputation. In the meantime Richard turned ten. The diagnosis was simple enough: incurable idiocy.

Day centres were not really intended for such cases; a closed institution would normally be considered. I had already learned as a child that an 'idiot' is like an enchanted prince, and that all depended on encouraging the prince's splendour to shine through by believing in it? After a maze of opposition from the authorities had been overcome, Richard joined our day centre. The boy took no notice of us but, in his permanent restlessness, wandered through the rooms with short, mincing steps. To make him sit down for a meal or anything else had been equally impossible at home. Hands on his hips he walked around from morning until evening between the children as if they were pieces of furniture.

This child, who will never again be well, was fortunate nevertheless in that he responded to everything the home could offer him. After half a year Richard could sit quietly at the table, hold the hands offered him when standing in a circle, sing a few notes and babble a few syllables. At Christmas was able to present his mother with a letter-folder with edges sewn by himself in colourful threads. And, most important of all, he would look at our mouths, eyes and hands to try and guess what we intended or wanted.

Parents sometimes react in unexpected ways. Richard came from a good, middle class home. Considered unable to ever do anything at all, now this boy began to set the table, remove the kettle from the stove before it had whistled, and to wipe the freshly polished floor with a rag to bring out a shine, after his mother had finished. In his newly awakened urge to be active Richard now disturbed the peace, his mother complained to us. I had to ask myself: are not parents, even those of healthy children, of the opinion that white tablecloths and shiny floors are more important than their children's peace of mind?

Pilo

In the backstreets of a large English port there lived a prostitute who gave birth to a son from one of the many sailors. Because she did not know what to do with a child, and he was handicapped, she left him in one of the slum's dark tenement yards. Pilo did not perish there. Rubbish was thrown out of the windows, and he soon learned to suck the remains from banana skins, and to chew dry crusts. He crawled on all fours and ate with his mouth to the ground like an animal. Welfare workers did not dare enter this particular slum area, but when Pilo, the 'little animal', was eight years old a miracle nevertheless took place when a pitying soul handed him over to the authorities.

At that time I visited the anthroposophical home which had taken him in. Pilo had already been there three months, but could not at all relate to tables, chairs, electric lights and, above all, to human contacts. At grace before meals the children held hands in a circle. So that Pilo could join in, my son, who was his teacher, had carved two pretty pieces of wood which Pilo then clasped in his hands and held out to the children sitting to his left and right, instead of holding hands. In this way he was part of the circle, yet did not have to shrink back because of the physical contact with other people.

He was given a spoon, and during the meal I watched as perhaps twenty times Pilo put his hand in the soup, and my son kindly told him: 'Pilo, remember your spoon, please.'

Pilo took up his spoon and my son said: 'Thank you, Pilo.'

And the same thing would start again after two mouthfuls: 'Remember your spoon, please; thank you, Pilo; remember your spoon, please; thank you, Pilo . . .' endlessly. Then my son looked at the large dining-room clock and said to me. 'It's nearly twelve o'clock exactly, then you will see something very strange.'

The dining-room had large glass windows through which one could see out over meadows to the bay. Lots of steamers, sailing boats, even gigantic cruisers travelled back and forth in continuous movement before our eyes. Pilo sat with his back to the window. Naturally, he could not tell the time, but at twelve o'clock on the dot he hastily turned round and his tired, apathetic eyes came alive as he gazed intently: there on the wide bay of water a bright red police or fire boat shot by, as it did every day punctually at this hour. Pilo, who had known nothing but house walls, drains, and wet pavements, had fallen in love with the red boat. He had not once failed to turn round and stare at the red dot punctually at twelve! I cannot explain this occurrence, because I do not understand it myself. A hundred children continue eating indifferently, while in Pilo's confused and apathetic spirit a spark flares up in greeting to the first friend in his short life — a red boat.

There still remains to be said that Pilo's loose-living mother appeared, at first shy, critical and distant, but that with time, in the atmosphere of the home and impressed by Pilo's slow awakening, she felt the need to begin her life anew.

22

Epilogue

Whenever one enters a ward for the mentally disturbed one is struck by a certain uniformity — however individual their lives may be, their appearance is stereotyped, monotonous; something unreal and intangible hovers around these people. It is the same in all wards of the world as it is in hospitals — the crazy are set apart from the social stream; contourless, colourless, as if afloat.

On the other hand the world does not react uniformly. I have described my experiences in other countries; it is quite remarkable how the attitude towards the handicapped and insane differs from nation to nation. They behave just as differently as any individual in a given situation: disgusted, afraid, indifferent or truly sympathetic.

I have been lucky to have come into close contact — partly as colleague, partly as an attentive pupil — with doctors, curative teachers and ministers who demonstrated dedication for the sake of those patients whose personalities were buried beneath sickness. It is important that one is exposed to such examples. One could say that psychiatry, like music, equally requires talent and living example to be truly mastered. I have been able to learn from many wise exponents of my profession. They unobtrusively awakened in me a sense of the fundamental image of man, they wrought in my soul devotion and wonder. That which the little girl in the Snow White and Rose Red fairy tale instinctively perceived — the gold beneath the bearskin; the 'I' hidden by the shaggy coat of illness — that was no longer a mere notion but had become certainty.

Thus these sketches were born out of gratitude, and shall be dedicated to all those parents whose sons and daughters have become strangers to themselves, who will be helped whenever the ill ones are regarded with true insight.